COLQUHOUN, MILLER
& PARTNERS

Alan Colquhoun
& John Miller

Introduction by
Kenneth Frampton

RIZZOLI
NEW YORK

First published in the United States of America in 1988 by
RIZZOLI INTERNATIONAL PUBLICATIONS, INC.
597 Fifth Avenue, New York, NY 10017

Library of Congress Cataloguing-in-Publication Data

Colquhoun, Miller & Partners/with an introduction by Alan Colquhoun and John Miller;
    editor, Kenneth Frampton.
    ISBN 0–8478–0952–6:
    1. Colquhoun, Miller & Partners—Criticism and interpretation.
2. Architecture, Modern—20th century—Great Britain—Themes, motives.
3. Architecture—Great Britain—Themes, motives.
I. Frampton, Kenneth. II. Title: Colquhoun, Miller & Partners.
NA997.C65C6   1988
720'.92'2—dc19   88–4632
                                              CIP

Designed by Blackpool Design, New York
Set in type by Typogram Inc., New York
Printed and bound in the U.S.A.

FOREWORD

4   The publication of one's work provides the opportunity of a backward look at the work as a whole. Comparing the projects that we designed at the outset of the partnership in 1961 with our more recent work, it seems clear that there has been a development, though this is perhaps not easy to define.

The most tangible change has come in the type of commissions we have received. In the sixties, medium to large sized public commissions, particularly of schools and university buildings, were still common, and throughout this period our projects tended to be of this kind. For the next ten years our work was almost exclusively restricted to public housing. More recently, we have received several commissions for buildings (particularly museums) that have involved extensions and modifications to existing buildings of artistic or historical importance. These vicissitudes are similar to those of other practices, and have followed general economic and political trends in Europe.

Inevitably, these changes of function-type have involved changes of architectural focus. One of the most significant of these has been the change from seeing a new building as a self-contained entity, whose form is generated by criteria internal to the building itself (whether these are concerned with program, technique, or form), to the idea that a new building is part of an existing context (formal/spatial or cultural/historical). The problem of context, together with the related one of the public reception of architecture, has dominated architectural discourse during the last fifteen years or so. In our case, these preoccupations have been closely bound up with specific problems that have arisen in connection with public housing and extensions to existing buildings. In the area of public housing, in particular, we were brought face to face with a completely new set of problems. Designing infill housing in London, or housing ensembles in the new town of Milton Keynes, led to a very precise critique of certain aspects of the modernist tradition. Not only had

this tradition undermined the humane qualities of the existing urban pattern, but, by putting a premium on spatial and formal solutions associated with the structural frame, it had encumbered housing with an empty formalism and a spurious utopianism. It seemed, on the contrary, that in housing one was dealing with a type that had changed very little in the last 150 years, both in terms of use and construction, and that one was operating within an urban morphology that was functionally and structurally sound.

Perhaps the best way of seeing how such preoccupations have affected the direction of our work would be to examine it in terms of a particular concept—that of typology. The idea that historical precedent could be reduced to a typology of available forms has always been important to us. In Forest Gate High School and Royal Holloway College, for example, we developed plans in which large, centrally placed rooms gave a sense of orientation and hierarchy to complex buildings. These solutions were based on classical precedent, and attempted to counteract the tendency towards dispersal in buildings of similar type within the modernist tradition.

But, despite our interest in classical organization, we saw typology as subservient to more general modernist ideas. Our approach involved the classification of functions to create a logical system of formal hierarchies and symmetries, chiefly developed in the plan. Typology was important, but only on condition that it was able to be filtered through a process of abstraction that "cleansed" it of all figural or linguistic reference. In this attitude we were following the general principles of modernist abstraction.

A particular example—that of fenestration—will make it possible to follow the evolution in our work from this approach to one that places more value on forms that make reference to traditional figures. In our earlier work, the fenestration of a building was thought of as determined more by rational analysis than by precedent or convention. This resulted, as at Forest Gate or Holloway College, in strip or panel windows spanning between structural walls or columns. (Of course, by the time we came to make use of it, this device had already become a convention, to which had been attached its own burden of meanings.) In our more recent work, our approach to this problem has become more open. We do not now regard the traditional "window" as having "bad" associations, and needing to be reduced to the status of a fissure between two solids. Rather, we see it as an element with a complex set of uses and meanings, none of which has absolute priority over any other, and some of which are derived from traditional practice. This concept of the window is closely related to another element—the wall. The window is now thought of as modifying the wall in which it appears, and as entering into a dialogue with it while the wall itself has the function of forming spatial boundaries and creating surfaces, in contrast to the frequent modernist practice of dissolving the wall by means of open frameworks or filters.

This broadening of the concept of typology to include facade elements involves a new awareness of the problem of architectural language. Instead of being based on the idea of a single language that is required to reflect "the spirit of the age" and seeks an architecture in which the area of choice is reduced to a minimum, our recent work recognizes the existence of a multiplicity of "language games" that may vary according to circumstance. In certain projects we have explored that area of architectural form that lies ambiguously between the type and the model. To some extent this has been dictated by the problem of designing in a strong architectural context. The extent to which a project borrows its language from its context depends on the degree of unity or heterogeneity in the context itself and cannot be reduced to a rule. In heterogeneous contexts there is likely to be greater freedom to develop original idioms. In "strong" contexts, on the contrary, the existing unity can easily be destroyed by the

introduction of an aggressively different language, and the gap between the type and the model will tend to diminish.

Although the problem of language is particularly obvious in the case of additions or infills, it is in reality a general problem, once it is admitted that no building can be considered to be a tabula rasa. This necessarily involves the attempt at a redefinition of the role played by language in modern design generally. This problem, however, cannot be solved by laying down precepts of a general kind and then following them mechanically. It can only be approached concretely. To give a particular example of such an approach from our own work, several housing projects designed for the new town of Milton Keynes are more or less unconstrained in terms of architectural context, but they have been influenced by earlier projects designed for more positive contexts. It is by this pragmatic route that we have arrived at a language that seems appropriate to the problem of housing in general. This process, which is the reverse of "logical," and which depends on basing general solutions on more specific ones, seems to respond to the present situation and to offer a possible approach to the problem of language.

Beyond these pragmatic strategies, however, there exists a more general body of ideas, which tend to emerge in discussion whenever a particularly intractible problem arrives. These ideas take their nourishment partly from the critical discourse of the last few years, in which many of the cliches of modernist theory have been put in question, and partly from an older discourse, of which the modern movement was itself the outcome. This older discourse arose from the need to redefine architecture after the dissolution of classical tradition and the "discovery" of ahistorical relativism. The problem raised in this discourse, which was not definitively solved by the modern movement, is how to reconstitute architecture as a quasi-autonomous practice, when all the traditional habits of design and construction have been lost. It

6   is a problem each architect has to try to solve in his own way, even if the ultimate aim is to find a universal solution.

For us, one of the most important aspects of this problem is to find the just relationship between language on the one hand, and function and structure on the other — between what might be called (following a traditional philosophical distinction) the secondary characteristics of a building and its substance.

This question formed one of the main subjects of debate in the 19th century, and it has returned today in a new form. It is here (to return to our original theme) that a typological approach can be fruitful, since such an approach must be concerned with forms that have evolved historically from the needs of function and construction and that are never, in the last analysis, either arbitrary or merely decorative.

Alan Colquhoun and John Miller

BIOGRAPHICAL NOTE
The Colquhoun & Miller partnership was formed in 1961. Richard Brearley became partner in 1975 and Su Rogers in 1987. The same year the firm's name was changed to Colquhoun, Miller & Partners.

Looking back over a quarter of a century, the most remarkable thing about the work of Colquhoun, Miller and Partners is the basic consistency of their approach; a fidelity to principle that except for the occasional vagrant work, we may recognize as their house style. By style, in this instance, one looks to a fundamental method rather than something concerned solely with appearance. Nonetheless, a certain shift in taste over the past decade or so has led to the introduction of more traditional architectural features, such as pitched roods and pierced windows, even if these have been incorporated without there being much change in the way in which the spatial body of a building is conceived. This constant approach is most evident perhaps in the parallel that may be drawn between the Forest Gate High School (1965) and the Oldbrook Estate in Milton Keyes (1982). In both we encounter a comparable cellular structure and a system of plan rotation, not to mention the similar use of an incomplete figure to define a public exterior.

Forest Gate High School was to establish the authority of the practice with remarkable decisiveness and, in looking back, one is astonished to find how mature this work was and how, in some respects, it amounted to a summation of the craft line within the modern movement. This is most evident perhaps in its feeling for post-Berlagian, Dutch and German brick construction at its best, in its awareness of the pre-war building of W. M. Dudok and Mies van der Rohe and in its regard for the monumental brickwork of Louis Kahn as manifest in his Yale Gallery and Richards Research Laboratories.

In its distribution of enclosed cells about a square assembly hall and in the setting of the whole plan composition within a virtual square, one may say that the Forest Gate High School already synthesizes a critical attitude toward the excesses of the avant garde. From this point of view, the work obviously has its rightful place in the annals of the British New Brutalist movement (see Reyner Banham's *The New Brutalism*). A comparison with Alison and Peter Smithson's Hunstanton School in Norfolk (1949–54) is instructive, for while the two works are equally anti-empirical in terms of their formal layout and geometric order, the Smithsons' school is evidently a much more polemical piece and its didactic abrasiveness (exposed plumbing, etc) so characteristic of the Brutalist ethic, is decidedly absent in the discrete detailing of the Forest Gate School. Even the inter-crosswall, classroom fenestration, which, as the architects pint out, was in accordance with the *de rigueur* spandrel windows of the period, was offset at Forest Gate by the disposition of the solid brick walls with pierced windows that were deployed for the auxiliary parts of the building.

This plastic, asymmetrical manner was an integral part of the Brutalist approach; it is already there in the in-fill housing exhibited by the Smithsons and James Stirling at CIAM-X conference held in Aix-en Provence in 1955 and it recurs as a theme in the residential work of Colquhoun and Miller, above all their project for a farm in Wales (1972) or in their Fenny Stratford infill housing of 1978.

The chemistry building at the Royal Holloway College (1970) was even more typological in its method, not only in terms of the absolute axiality of its layout but also with regard to the systematic "double" structural grid that permeates the entire complex and provides space for the service ducts running throughout the open laboratory space. Two precedents seem to have had a direct bearing on this building; on the one hand, the standard tartan grid, developed by Leslie Martin as a general strategy for servicing the new science facilities then being built under the auspices of the University Grants Commission, and on the other, the general inspiration of Vanburgh's baroque architecture, particularly pertinent here, where the building cascaded down a rather picturesque site, flanked by the Gothic pinnacles of the late nineteenth-century pile to which it was an addition.

8 Although there is no direct link, other than Giulio Carlo Argan's thesis on typology, first published in English in 1962, the Royal Holloway College laboratory is highly reminiscent of the rationalist paradigms then being proposed by the leading architects of the Italian Tendenza, namely Aldo Rossi and Giorgio Grassi.

That the first half of the 1970s was an experimental interlude in the evolution of the practice seems to be borne out by a number of rather empirical diminutive "high-tech" works that are projected and realized by the firm between 1973 and 1976. Of these, the two most provocative are the twin houses designed for the riverside site known as Pillwood, in Cornwall; the first, being realized by John Miller and Su Rogers for their own use and the second being an unrealized house projected for a graphic designer. Pillwood 1 (1976) employs off-the-peg standard greenhouse glazing and GRC panels for the enclosure of rudimentary week-end accommodation. The planning is both informal and transformable so that the spatial sub-division can be re-organized according to the number of guests, sliding partitions enabling one to increase or decrease the number of cells according to the density of occupation. This transformation is further facilitated by a cylindrical spiral stair that affords access from the various sleeping quarters to a common bathroom. As in the chemistry laboratory, the formal principle is an absolutely axial composition descending a slope. This house is the most consistent exploration of the high-tech syntax that the firm has conducted to date. It manifests a higher level of architectural resolution that either the Melrose Avenue or the Welbourne Road community centers that were employ similar materials and forms in conjunction with long-span, space-frame construction.

It is regrettable that Pillwood 2 (1972) was never built for in many respects it represents a subtle synthesis that possesses considerable potential for future development. Not only is Pillwood 2 spatially layered as it descends the slope from a pedestrian entry at high level, but it also combines heavy-weight masonry construction with light steel fenestrations and decking in a particularly appropriate way. This juxtaposition is played out at a micro-scale in the top lit entrance corridor that, covered with a mono-pitched glass monitor, passes through the house as a spatial slot, separating the thick storage wall at the back of the site from the main body of the house facing on to the river. The steel framing of the sliding, living-room windows opening to the terrace is nicely echoed by the light tubular steel pergola that links the building to the tubular ballustrading of the terrace itself.

With their Oldbrook Estate, built in Milton Keynes in 1982, the architects began to incorporate paradigms taken from the Arts and Crafts pre-history of the modern movement. In this instance the point of departure was the garden city planning evolved by Raymond Unwin and Barry Parker and more directly the housing work of M. H. Baillie-Scott; above all ghis Court in Hampstead Garden Suburb of 1909 and his unbuilt Plot 400, Meadway designed for the same suburb of a year before. The main borrowing from Baillie-Scott lay in the pavilionized courtyard form and in the upper story windows, set tight under the eaves. By any standards Oldbrook Estate is a remarkable achievement since it was to maintain quality while satisfying the demand that the expression be popularly accessible, namely the bureaucratic insistence on pitched roofs and pierced windows. Aside from the axiality of the car access courts much of this last depends on the inflected use of traditional features, such as brick string courses, brick-on-end lintols and cills, square paneled garage doors and over hanging Italianate eaves. Yet another Arts and Crafts reference is introduced in the Mackintosh-like, gridded bay windows that terminate the ends of the terraces; a feature that somewhat misleadingly suggests the presence of a stair hall. Be this as it may, the vertical gridded form serves to turn and terminate the ends of the twin courtyard wings.

While the in-fill housing produced for Shrubland Road and Albion Drive in 1984 was overly Neoclassic following the tone set by the 1840's Hackney Street fabric into which it was inserted, comparable double -fronted, in-fill villas for Church Crescent. Hackney, also dating from 1984, was treated in a Neo-Italianate manner comparable to the strategy adopted in the Oldbrook Estate. A similar Neo-Italianate approach had been evolved five years before in the Caversham Road/Gaisford Street, in-fill complex where a conscious play was established between traditional and modern forms. The subtlety of this game merits analytical comment. It is worth mentioning the combined moves made by the architects, in completing the missing half of a semidetached nineteenth-century villa. There were (1) extending the original roof over the new apartments, (2) establishing a certain parallel between the string courses, proportion and scale of the old villa and the new addition (3) arranging for the bedrooms of the upper duplex to have cantilevered side-lit, bulkheads and (4) counterpointing the fenestration of the old house by introducing a different but sympathetic pattern of solids and voids. As one passes through the lot to the Gaisford Street frontage this ambiguous syntax is transformed into a more modern abstract expression that is to say, geometric forms and orthogonal window openings that are more silent in a Loosian sense. They are, as it were, nothing more than the well proportioned outcome of the logic of design and its construction. The loss of the mid-block community center is to be regretted in that it would have mediated between the different modes of expression adopted in each street frontage.

 The Two Mile Ash housing estate, completed at Milton Keynes in 1984, closes this particular cycle of low-rise housing and the adoption here of an exclusively semidetached housing typology directly reflects the increasing privatization of the society since, unlike the Oldbrook Estate, these houses have been produced for sale. This loss of formal and symbolic continuity no doubt accounts for the covered carports and for the linking pergolas that not only shade the access but also serve to tie the houses together and create clearly defined sectors of exterior space. Once again the language employed evokes the modern garden city ethos of the 1920s and 1930s.

Housing of a more urban order was to be realized in the nine story double-fronted slab that the firm saw realized in Hornsey Lane in 1980 and in their more recent IBA Housing Competition entry of 1987, which comprised continuous perimeter block units of heights varying from five to seven stories. The Hornsey Lane slab is basically a stack of two-room apartments. The building was something of a prototype since it was planned in such a way as to provide alternatively either for childless married couples or for two single persons sharing the same unit.

In terms of high-rise housing, the most experimental work pursued by the firm to date was undoubtedly the Millbank Housing competition of 1976 that in certain respects can be regarded as their most American work since the *parti* is reminiscent of the work of John Hejduk. To conceive of the complex in terms of three blocks that are respectively circular, square and triangular in plan is apparently to adopt an extremely formalist format, one that, the optimization of river views notwithstanding, flies in the face of the empirical tradition to which the office otherwise adheres. This much is surely evident from the apartment plans that seem a little forced in places, particularly where the living space afforded by different type plans varies so greatly in terms of both floor area and shape.

The refurbishing of the Whitechapel Art Gallery, competed in 1986, has led to a fundamental change in the character of the commissions now being received by the office for the practice has since been invited to participate in a series of limited museum competitions including the National Gallery, London, the Staedel Institute of Art, Frankfurt, the Fitzwilliam Museum, Cambridge and the Messepalast, Vienna. As far as the current reputation of the office is concerned, however, the Whitechapel Gallery remains a seminal and decisive work. Indeed, one may think of it as culminating a particular period of development; in the first place because the more recent museums projected by the office have assumed a Neoclassical stance, in the second, because the Whitechapel was to afford the greatest possible scope for the office penchant of reinterpreting the late Arts and Crafts line; the job entailing the rearrangement of a canonical piece built to the designs of C. H. Townsend and dating from the turn of the century. The fact that Townsend was part of the mainstream of the British Art Nouveau was of consequence since it meant that the form of the Whitechapel had been pre-determined by the cultural program evolved by Lethaby and Voysey and extending to include the work of such architects as Townsend and C. R. Mackintosh.

Miller's personal affinity for Mackintosh permeates this rehabilitation and addition without ever leading him into pastiche. This constant respect, as it were, is manifest in the extreme discretion with which the building has been detailed. Thus while no attempt was made to mimic the Celtic-cum-Richardsonian character of Townsend's terracotta and stone facade or to recall directly Mackintosh's attenuated grids and screens, the refurbishing is nonetheless highly attuned to the specific cultural context of the building. This empathetic response is largely attained through the extensive use of brick soldier courses throughout the new facade (destined to be more fully revealed in the future) and through the introduction of such neo-Celtic devices as the gridded clerestorey to the large bow-window of the refectory or the square gridded relief paneling of the matt black doors that appear throughout the rebuilt interior.

This *règpètition differente*, to quote Roland Barthes, attains its apotheosis in the design of the stairs with their light tubular metal handrails and square marble inserts set into terrazzo treads. While this is as delicate and as graphics as anything that Mackintosh ever designed, it results in an altogether more modern gestalt, for one can hardly miss the nautical metaphor that is present throughout the public circulation, from the horizontal tubular balustrading to the circular light fittings. This is not however the familiar Corbusian transposition of marine detailing to civic building. It is, if anything, closer to the Art Deco sensibility of Rob Mallet-Stevens and to the disciplined expressionism of Erich Mendlesohn and Oliver Hill than to the didactic functionalism of either Purism or the New Objectivity.

It may be imagined that a similar spirit will pervade the new faculty building that is about to be constructed for the Royal College of Art, London, where the Celtic spirit crops up again in the attenuated proportions of the studio fenestration, which is as evocative of Jospeh Hoffman as of Mackintosh. And yet not withstanding the breadth of the culture to which this work aspires it is interesting to note the extent to which the Glasgow School of Art remains a constant reference in the history of the Royal College, since the Kensington Gore building designed by J. Cadbury Brown in the mid-fifties, made a patent homage to Mackintosh's masterwork in the profiling of its roof.

Within the constraints of this Celtic frame much has been done to relate the new facade of the new building to the scale and texture of the Jay Mews frontage. This is no doubt accounts for the Neo-Italianate treatment of the brick elevation and for the rhythm and scale of the grouped window openings. Aside from this the interior amounts to a top-lit inner court about which all the new studies are ingeniously arranged in one way or another. What is more creditable in this is the skill with which the existing tripartite cross-wall construction of the Queen's Gate frontage has been related back to the centralized *parti* of the interior. The amount of ingenuity that this has entailed in both section and plan can well be imagined from the precise placement of the ramps and the positioning of the various escape stairs.

The more recent designs for museums would seem to introduce a rupture within the craft tradition of the office and this is more noticeable in the spatial strategies adopted rather than in the appearance of the works themselves. Nothing is perhaps more indicative of this than the *ensuite* planning of the principal galleries in the National Gallery project. Here every top-lit room seems to have been obsessively rendered within the Neoclassical rubric, as a complete room in itself, entailing a certain amount of *pochè* or lost space. In other words the envelope and the general *parti* are one thing and the resultant volumetric hierarchy is quite another. The price of this schismatic approach seems to be a loss of spatial energy and freedom, although its presence is not automatically anti-modernist, viz the work of Aalto.

The reasons for this recourse to the Beaux-Arts are no doubt as complex as they are symptomatic. On the one hand of course it may be quite simply read as a direct function of the given context, a response to the context of the average nineteenth-century museum complex, corresponding to the previous response to an Arts and Crafts heritage. On the other, this move might be seen as having ideological causes, particularly when one takes into account the general loss of faith in the modern project, combined with the ongoing Neoconservative modernization of society that is as ruthless in contemporary Britain as anywhere else. Surely today's somewhat overwrought concern for architectural autonomy and for the limits of architecture is extremely double-edged, particularly when it leads to the inhibition of creativity. Would we not be better advised to follow Auguste Perret and to look to the Neoclassic for its exposed trabeated rhythm rather than for the Beaux-Arts tradition of *pochè*? In spite of these doubts it is possible to claim that while the general image of the work of Colquhoun, Miller and Partners has changed over time, the fundamental priority given to a typological point of view has remained constant.

Kenneth Frampton

PROJECT DATA

This is a complete list of all projects designed by Colquhoun, Miller & Partners

PROJECT	CLIENT/DESCRIPTION	DATE	TEAM	CONSULTANTS
FOREST GATE HIGH SCHOOL London	London Boroughof West Ham	1961–1965	Paul Yarker	*QS:* Monk & Dunstone *M/E:* Wingfield-Bowles *St/Eng:* F.J. Samuely & Ptr.
GALLERY FOR PRECOLUMBIAN ART Belsize Park Gardens, London	Miss Kemper	1964		
HOUSE Surrey	Mr. B. Lodge (Project)	1964		
OFFICE CONVERSION City of London	Reuters	1964	Geoffrey Wigfall	
CHEMISTRY BUILDING Royal Holloway College Egham, Surrey	Royal Holloway College	1965–1971	David Bryan, Chris Cross , Tony Musgrove, Ed Jones	*QS:* Monk & Dunstone *M/E:* Dale & Ewbank *St/Eng:* F.J. Samuely & Ptr.
LIBRARY Eaton Place, London	Mr. B. Drummond (Project)	1966		
SHOP CONVERSION Covent Garden, London	Miss Christina Smith	1966		
HOUSE Surrey	Mr. Leslie McCombie (Project)	1967		
PRINT AND MAP SHOP London	Weinreb & Douwma	1968–1969	Madhu Sarin	*QS:* Monk & Dunstone
CLIFTON CANON LEE School Yorkshire	West Riding of Yorkshire	1970–1973	Dougal Campbell, David Dryan, Roger Barcroft	*QS:* H. Trinick & Ptrs. *M/E:* N.I.F.E.S. *St/Eng:* F.J. Samuely & Ptr.
KINGSGATE Miles Cloverdale Colville & Brackenbury Primary Schools London	G.L.C.	1970–1971		Kingsgate: *M/E:* F. J. Baynes & Co. *St/Eng:* F. Y,. Samuely & Ptr. Brackenbury *M/E:* GLC/ILEA
DERBY CIVIC HALL	Invited Competition	1970		
HOUSE CONVERSION Balcombe Street London	Durrants Hotel	1971	Alan Basing	
HOUSE CONVERSION Boston Place London	Durrants Hotel (Project)	1971		

PROJECT	CLIENT/DESCRIPTION	DATE	TEAM	CONSULTANTS
LOWER HOUSE FARM Wales	Mr. Lyman Dixon	1970–1973	Dougal Campbell	
PILLWOOD 1 Cornwall	Mr. & Mrs. Brumwell	1972–1975	Roger Barcroft	QS: Monk & Dunstone, Mahon & Scears St/Eng: A. Hunt Associates
PILLWOOD 2 Cornwall	Mr. John Raynes	1972	Simon Winstanley	
MELROSE AVENUE COMMUNITY CENTER Bletchley	Milton Keynes Development Corporation	1972–1974	Simon Winstanley, John Parker Russell Bevington	QS: Monk & Dunston M/E: John Bradley Assoc. St/Eng: F. J. Samueley & Ptr.
HOLIDAY CHALETS Aviemore, Scotland	Time Off Properties (Project)	1973	Roger Barcroft, Simon Whtistanley	
COCA-COLA FACTORY Milton Keynes	Invited Competition	1973		
OLD PERSONS HOME West Green Road London	London Borough of Haringey	1973–1976	Richard Brearley, Shinichi Tomoe	QS: Burrell Hayward & Budd M/E: L. B. of Haringey St/Eng: F. J. Samuely & Ptr.
WELBOURNE ROAD London	London Borough of Haringey	1974–1976	Simon Winstanley, Roger Barcroft	QS: Monk & Dunstone M/E: L. B. Haringey St/Eng: F. J. Samuely & Ptr.
HOUSING Fenny Stratford ("Backlands Site")	MKDC (Project)	1974	Simon Winstanley, Richard Brearley	QS: Monk & Dunstone
COLNAGHI'S London	Colnaghi's (Project)	1975	Simon Winstanley	
TWO MILE ASH Milton Keynes	MKDC (Project)	1975	Peter Roy, Simon Whitstanley	MKDC all consultancies
PRINCE ROAD Croydon	G.L.C. (Project)	1975	David Nixon	
HOUSING Caversham Road & Gaisford Street London	London Borough of Camden	1975–1979	Shinichi Tomoe, Innes Lamunière, David Nixon	QS: Robinson & Roods M/E: Dale & Goldfinger St/Eng: A. Hunt Assoc.
HOUSING Oldbrook II Milton Keynes	MKDC	1976–1982	John Hunter, Shinichi Tomoe	QS: Davis, Belfield & Everest M/E: Dale & Goldfinger St/Eng: F. J. Samuely & Ptr.

PROJECT	CLIENT/DESCRIPTION	DATE	TEAM	CONSULTANTS
HOUSING Fenny Stratford ("Corner Site")	MKDC	1976– 1978	Simon Winstanley, Innes Lamunière Shinichi Tomoe	*QS:* Monk & Dunstone *St/Eng:* A. Hunt Assoc.
HOUSING Millbank London	Open Competition	1977	Simon Winstanley, Peter Roy	
DADA & SURREALISM Exhibition London	Arts Council of Great Britain	1978	Innes Lamunière, Shinichi Tomoe	Graphic Designer: Edward Wright Exhibition Officer: Richard Francis
WHITECHAPEL ART GALLERY London	Trustees of Whitechapel Art Gallery	1978– 1985	Graham Smith, John Carpenter Norman Chang Peter Bernamont	*QS:* Brian Davis & Assoc. *M/E:* Steenson, Varming, Mulcahy & Partners *St/Eng:* F. J. Samuely & Ptr.
TAOSHEACH RESIDENCE & GUEST HOUSE Dublin	Open Competition	1979	Chris Hay, Peter Jones Sheila O'Donnell	*QS:* Davis Belfield & Everest
THEATRE WORKSHOP	R.H.C. (Project)	1979	Shinichi Tomoe	*QS:* Monk & Dunstone
THE ARTS OF BENGAL Exhibition London	Whitechapel Art Gallery in association with V & A	1979		
20TH CENTURY HOUSES Traveling Exhibition	Arts Council	1980	Sheila O'Donnell	
HOUSING Hornsey Lane London	London Borough of Haringey	1980	John Hunter, Shinichi Tomoe	*QS:* Monk & Dunstone *M/E:* L. B. of Haringey *St/Eng:* F. J. Samuely & Ptr.
HOUSING Shrubland Road & Albion Drive London	London Borough of Hackney	1981– 1984	John Hunter, Graham Smith Norman Chang	*QS:* Cross & Hall *St/Eng:* L. B. of Hackney
HOUSING Church Crescent London	London Borough of Hackney	1981– 1984	John Hunter, Graham Smith, Norman Chang	*QS:* Robinson Roods *M/E & St/Eng:* L. B. Hackney
HOUSING Central Milton Keynes	MKDC (Project)	1981		MKDC all consultancies
PICASSO'S PICASSOS Exhibition London	Arts Council Hayward Gallery	1981		

PROJECT	CLIENT/DESCRIPTION	DATE	TEAM	CONSULTANTS
SIR CHRISTOPHER WREN Exhibition London	Whitechapel Art Gallery	1982		
HOUSING Two Mile Ash Milton Keynes	MKDC	1982– 1984	John Carpenter, John Hunter	MKDC all consultancies
HOUSING Willen Park 2 Milton Keynes	MKDC	1983– 1985	Graham Smith	QS: Davis Belfield & Everest MKDC: all other consultancies
ADOLF LOOS Traveling Exhibition	Arts Council	1984		Selection of Material: Yahuda Safran, Wilfred Wang Graphic Design: Bernard Shaw
SHENLEY LODGE	MKDC	1985	John Carpenter	QS: Davis Belfield & Everest
MEDICAL RESEARCH LABORATORIES Addenbrookes Site Cambridge	Cambridge University Invited Competition First Prize	1986	Esmonde O'Briain, Norman Chang	QS: Davis Belfield & Everest M/E:d YRM Engineers St/Eng: A. Hunt Assoc.
GENERIC HOUSE	Ashby and Horner Team Contracts Ltd.	1986	Norman Chang	
GIBRALTAR EAST COAST DEVELOPMENT	Wimpey Trocom (Project)	1986	Graham Smith	QS: Davis Belfield & Everest St/Eng: Wallace Evans
THAMESMEAD HOUSING London	Thamesmead Development Corporation Invited Competition	1986	Norman Chang	Joint Venture with: William Sindall Ltd. BDP Landscape Architect: Janet Jack
NATIONAL GALLERY EXTENSION London	Trustees of the National Gallery Invited Competition	1986	Graham Smith, John Carpenter Norman Chang Avtar Lotay Patrick Theis Also assistants from RMJM	In association with RMJM Ltd., who provided consultanices Lighting: W. Bordass
STAEDEL INSTITUTE OF ART Frankfurt	Trustees of the Staedelsches Kunstinstitut Invited Competition Second Prize	1987	Patrick Theis, Tim Boyd Norman Chang	QS: Davis Belfield & Everest M/E: Ove Arup St/Eng: Ove Arup Landscaping: Janet Jack Liaison: Wlater Weiss
MESSEPALAST Vienna	Invited Competition	1987	Graham Smith, Nick Pham, Norman Chang	

WORK IN PROGRESS

PROJECT	CLIENT/DESCRIPTION	DATE	TEAM	CONSULTANTS
TATE GALLERY London	Trustees of the Tate Gallery	1986	Patrick Theis, Graham Smith, Esmonde O'Briain, Tim Boyd, Norman Chang	QS: Stern + Woodford *M/e:* Steenson, Varmig, Mulcahy & Partners *St/Eng:* F. J. Samuely & Ptr.
FITZWILLIAM MUSEUM Extension Cambridge	Trustees of the Fitzwilliam Museum	1986	Dean Smith, Patrick Theis, Esmonde O'Briain, Norman Chang	QS: Davis Belfield + Everest *M/E:* YRME *St/Eng:* A. Hunt Assoc.
ROYAL COLLEGE OF ART FACULTY BUILDING London	The Rector RCA	1986	Graham Smith, Simon Lanyon-Hogg, Dean Smith, Norman Chang, Tim Boyd Louise Cotter Patrick Theis	QS: Davis Belfield + Everest *M/E:* Ove Arup *St/Eng:* Ove Arup *Acoustics:* Ove Arup *Project Manager:* Dartington Management Services
REGENT STREET POLYTECHNIC London	Polytechnic of Central London	1986	Norman Chang	QS: Brian Davis + Assoc. Exhibition Consultant: Richard Allen Lighting: Arnold Chan
HOUSING Walnut Tree Site 3 Milton Keynes	Polytechnic of Central London	1986	Graham Smith	MKDC all consultancies
IBA HOUSING Berlin	IBA	1987	Nick Pham, Norman Chang, Graham Smith, Patrick Theis, Tom Boyd	
HOUSING Woodall House Site London	London Borough of Haringey	1987	Tim Boyd, Patrick Theis, Norman Chang	QS: Davis Belfield + Everest *M/E:* Dale & Goldfinger *St/Eng:* De Leuw, Chadwick, OhEocha
HAWLEY LOCK	Trevor Clarke (Project)	1987	Patrick Theis	

Previous page:
Forest Gate High School.
London, England, 1965.
Assembly Hall interior.

Forest Gate High School.
London, England, 1965.
Exterior from playground.

*Print and Map Shop
for Weinreb & Douwma.
London, England, 1969.
Interior.*

Chemistry Building,
Royal Holloway College.
Egham, Surrey, England, 1970.
Exterior.

Chemistry Building,
Royal Holloway College.
Egham, Surrey, England, 1970.
Interior of entrance lobby.

Pillwood 1.
Cornwall, England, 1975.
Exterior.

Housing, Caversham Road.
London, England, 1979.
Exterior.

Housing, Gaisford Street.
London, England, 1979.
Exterior.

Housing, Hornsey Lane.
London, England, 1980.
Exterior.

Housing, Oldbrook 2.
Milton Keynes, England, 1982.
Prospect.

26

*Housing, Shrubland Road
and Albion Drive.
London, England, 1984.
Exterior.*

*Housing, Church Crescent.
London, England, 1984.
Exterior.*

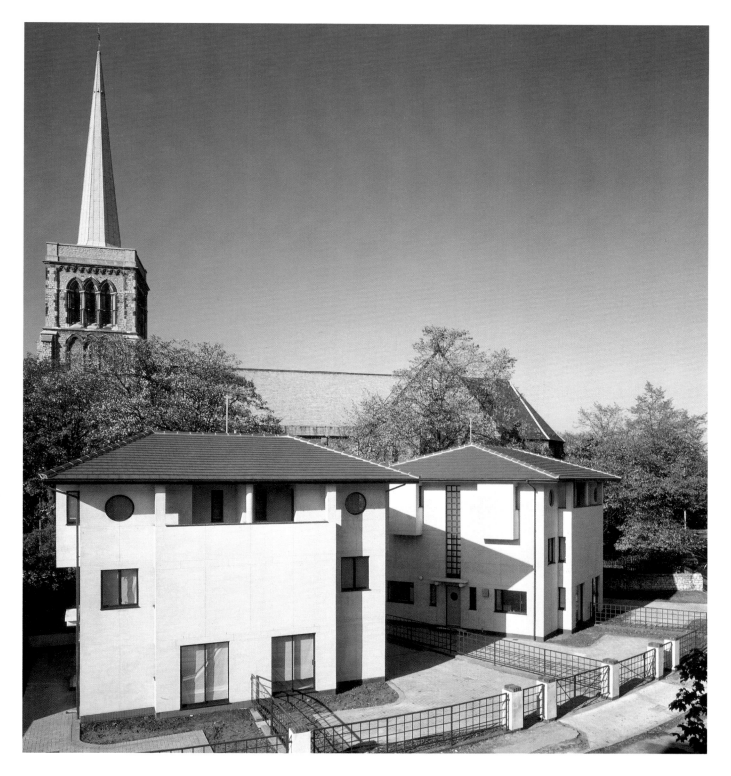

Whitechapel Art Gallery.
London, England, 1985.
Exterior from Angel Alley

Whitechapel Art Gallery.
London, England, 1985.
Lower Gallery interior.

32

Whitechapel Art Gallery.
London, England, 1985.
Interior view of Upper Gallery.

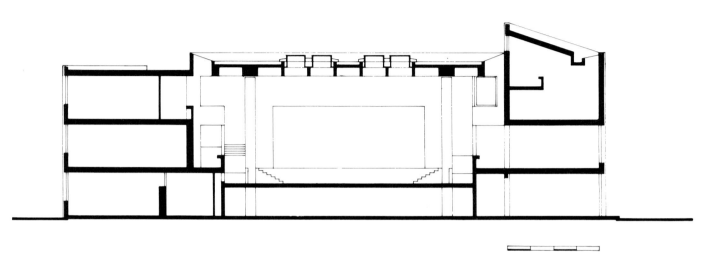

1

The program called for a mixed secondary school for 780 pupils, comprising 33 classrooms, an Assembly Hall, a dining room, two gymnasia, and three workshops. The school was to be built on a restricted urban site, and a three story structure was adopted to release as much space as possible for outdoor play.

The heart of the school is the Assembly Hall, which rises through all three stories and is surrounded by open, stepped corridors, giving access to all the classrooms. A continuous skylight articulates the Assembly Hall roof from the classrooms, flooding the corridors with light and creating the impression of an atrium. This arrangement is related to the schools built by the London County Council in the late 19th century, which were always planned around double height Halls.

The gymnasia and the workshops are accommodated in a separate block, connected to the main school by a bridge. The entire complex is circumscribed within a square. Tiled forecourts act as outdoor anterooms to the main pupils' entrance.

The school is constructed in load-bearing brickwork, with red facings. The window frames are in wood, painted white.

1   *Section.*

2 *Staff and visitor's entrance.*

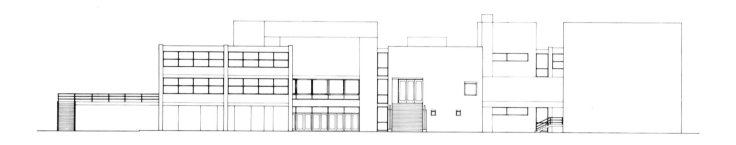

3

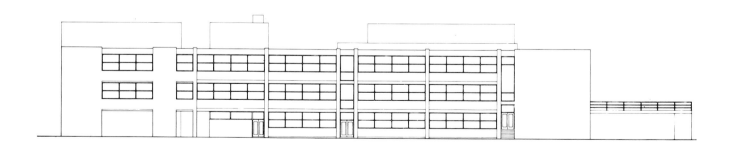

4

1 Playground
2 Caretaker

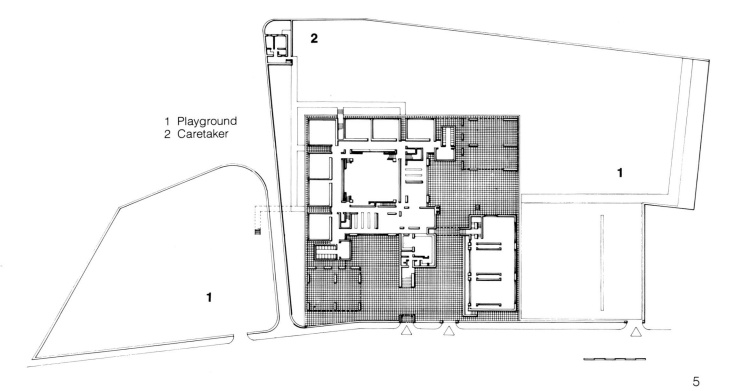

5

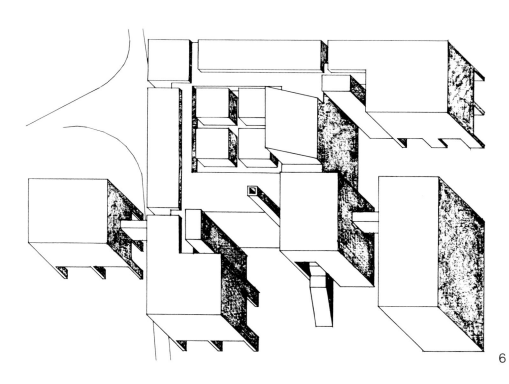

6

38

8

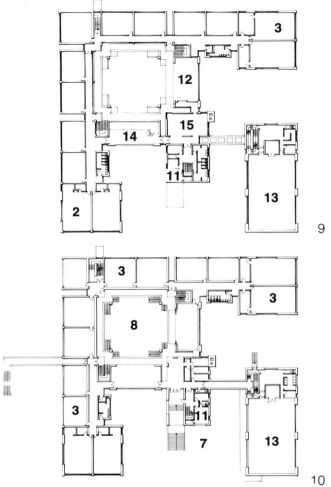

9

10

1 Playspace
2 Covered Play
3 Classrooms
4 Cloaks and Childrens Entrance
5 Dining and Kitchen
6 Workshops
7 Entrance for Community
  Functions and Staff
8 Assembly Hall
9 Stage
10 Music Room
11 Staff
12 Upper Part of Stage
13 Gymnasium
14 Library
15 Playground

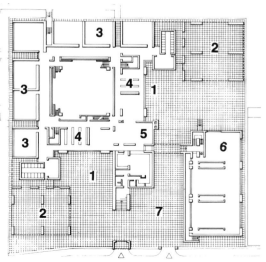

11

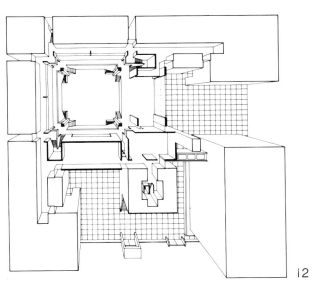

12

13

CHEMISTRY BUILDING

Royal Holloway College
Egham Surrey   1970

1

The program for the chemistry building consisted of four teaching laboratories, six research laboratories, two lecture theaters, offices, a library, and workshops.

The building was part of a program of expansion within the park-like grounds of the original 19th-century college.

The site slopes steeply, and the building is planned with the main entrance off a pedestrian mall at the upper end, and a service entrance off a service road at the lower end.

The accommodation is divided into two identical complexes, one overlapping the other, and both sharing a service core. In each complex, two sky-lit teaching laboratories occupy a central position at ground level and are ringed and bridged by research laboratories and offices on the second floor, to form a single academic unit. The library and lecture theaters are directly related to the entrance lobby.

Continuous loggias, following the slope of the ground, form a covered walk along both sides of the building and mediate between the laboratories and the natural surroundings.

The structure consists of a reinforced concrete frame, and is finished in smooth-faced concrete, infilled with aluminum and glass curtain walls. The ducts supplying services to the laboratories are integrated into a matrix of split beams and columns.

1 *Main entrance at night.*
2 *Covered walkway.*

3 *View of covered walkway.*
4 *Corner view.*
5 *Cross section.*

4

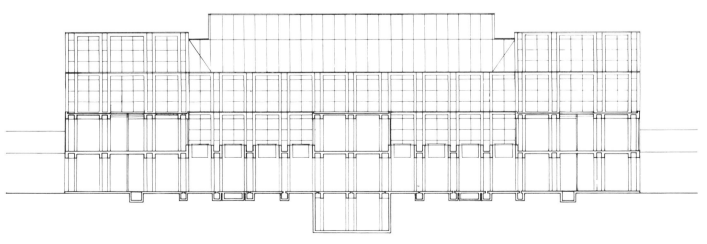

44

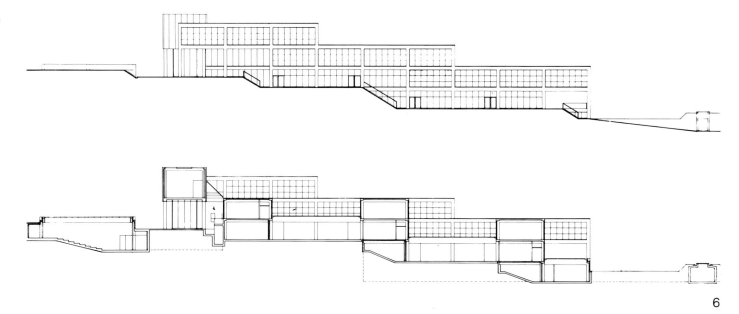

6

7

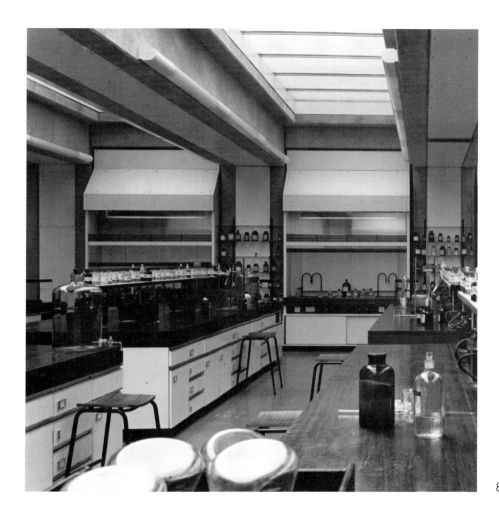

45

8

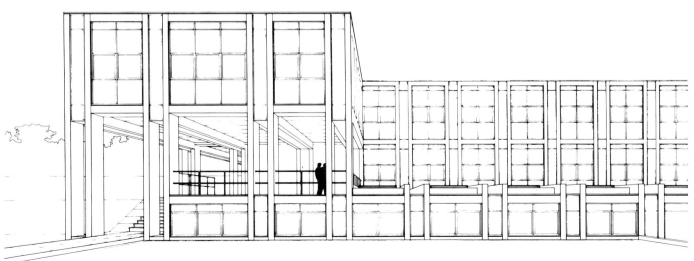

9

10 *View of entrance ramp.*
11 *Axonometric.*
12 *View of entrance lobby.*

10

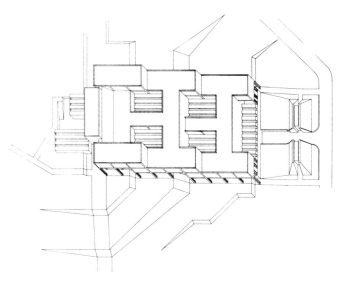

11

48

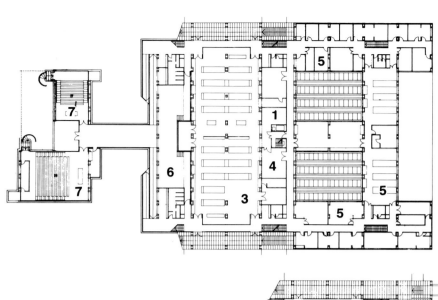

13

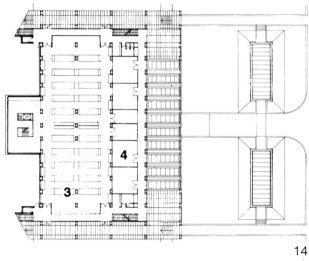

14

13 *Level 3 plan.*
14 *Level 2 plan.*
15 *Level 1 plan.*

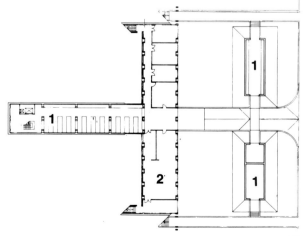

15

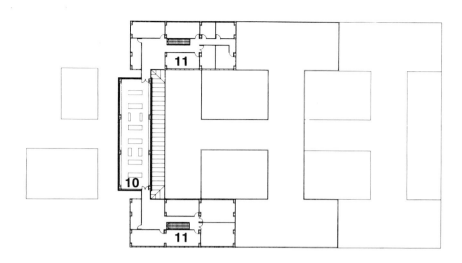

16

1 Stores
2 Workshops
3 Teaching Labs
4 Ancillary Labs
5 Research Labs
6 Plant Room

7 Lecture Theaters
8 Seminars
9 Main Entrance
10 Library
11 Social Rooms and Offices

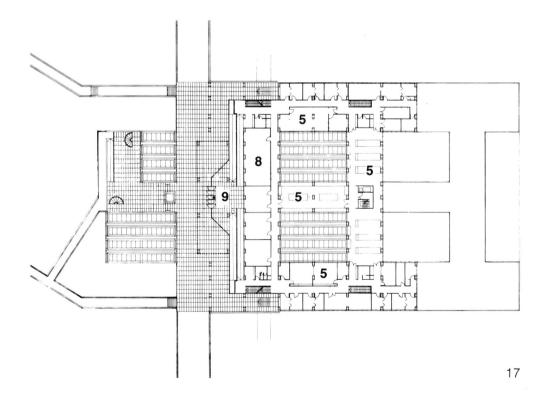

17

16 *Level 5 plan.*
17 *Level 4 plan.*

The program called for additions to an existing secondary school, including ten classrooms, a gymnasium, offices for teaching staff, a pupils' entrance, and cloakrooms. The linear elements of the program are wrapped around the volume of the gymnasium, into which there are views from the upper level corridor.

The structure consists of a steel frame, with precast concrete second floor slab and woodwool roof decking. The frame is clad in corrugated steel sandwich panels, and a steel window and spandrel system.

1 *Gymnasium.*   51
2 *View of pupils' entrance.*

2

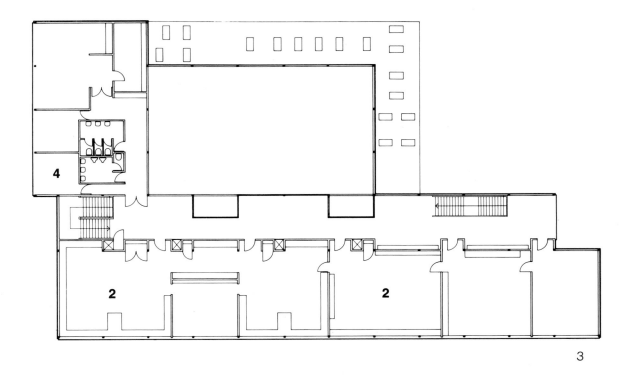

3

1 Main Entry   3 Gymnasium
2 Classroom   4 Administration

3   *Second floor plan.*
4   *First floor plan.*
5   *Longitudinal sections.*
6   *Site plan.*

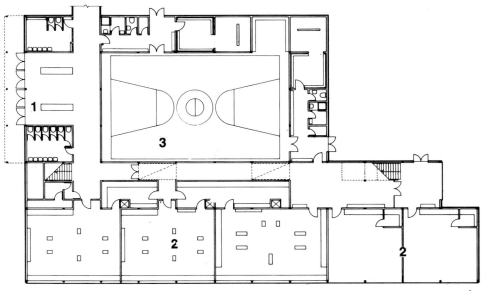

4

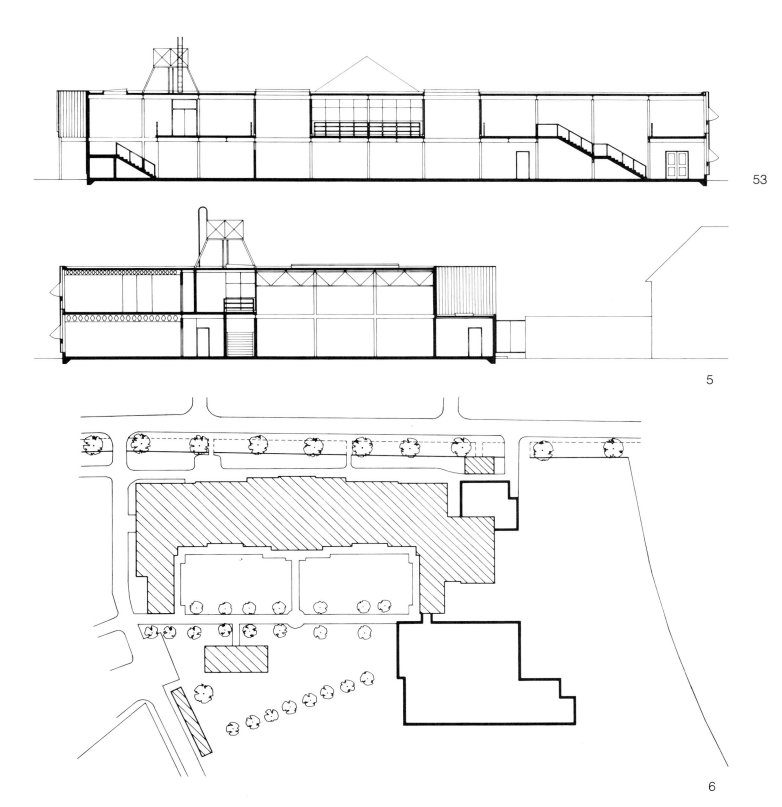

53

5

6

MEDICAL RESEARCH LABORATORIES

Addenbrookes Site
Cambridge   1986

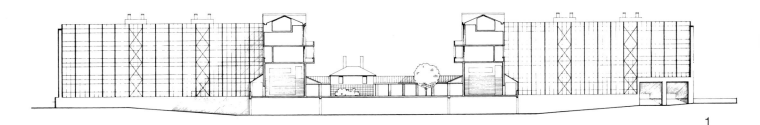

1

The competition conditions asked for a two-stage proposal, the first being for the immediate construction of new departments of Pharmacology and Biotechnology, the second being for a future department of Biochemistry. The site is near the center of Cambridge.

The solution consisted of linear blocks arranged to create a large three-sided courtyard off which all the departments would eventually be entered.

The laboratories occupied the major part of the building, on four stories. All laboratory floors were organized according to a standard section, the offices occupying the street frontage, and ducted and piped services running in a double glazed wall on the opposite face. The space between these two zones provided the maximum possible area for flexible laboratory layout.

Externally, the fenestration of the office spaces was adjusted to the domestic scale of the neighboring buildings, while the fully glazed and more technologically explicit surfaces faced onto the private part of the site.

1   *Elevations.*
2   *Cut-away axonometric showing typical laboratory.*

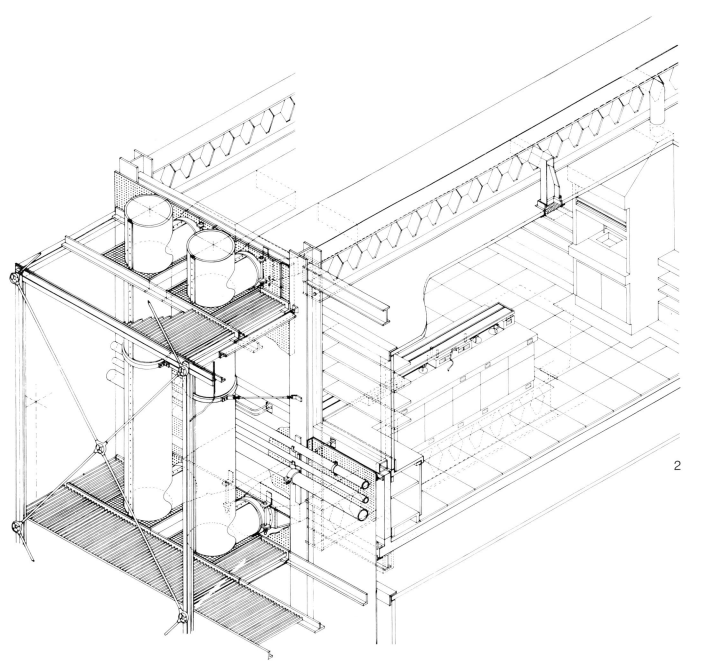

2

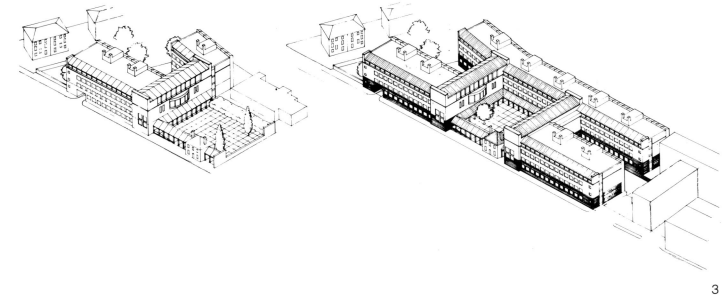

3

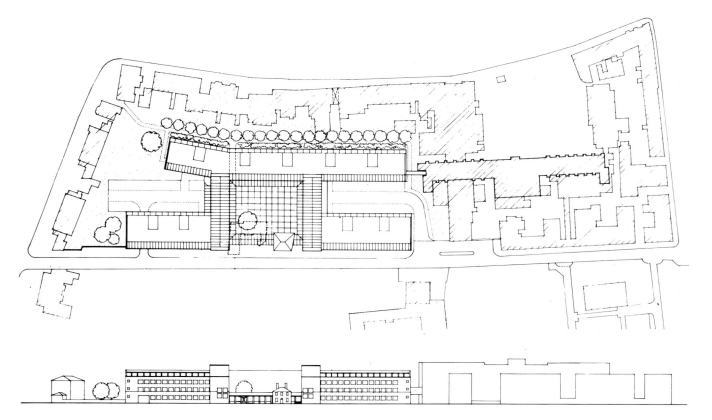

4

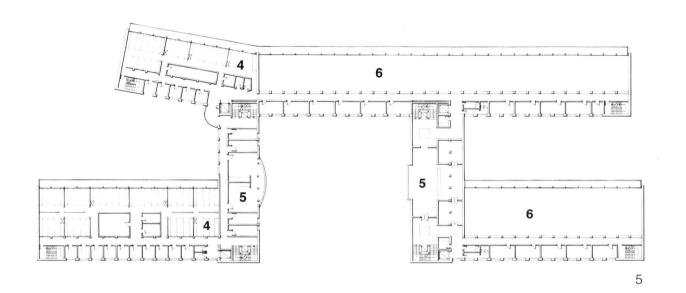

5

1 Entrance   4 Laboratories
2 Existing Lodge   5 Library
3 Lecture Hall   6 Future Labs

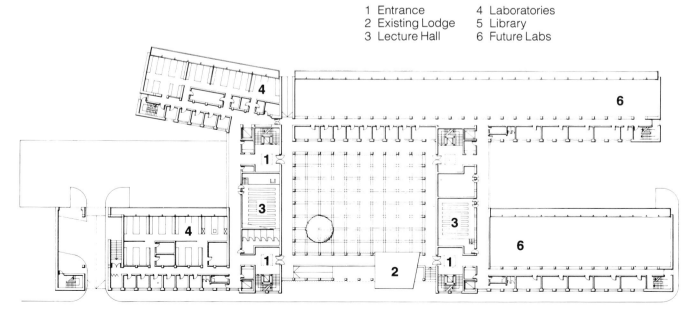

6

58 The site is bounded by Queensgate to the west and Jay Mews to the east. The Queensgate frontage is made up of buildings of historical interest and the site as a whole is within a conservation area.

The program calls for new studios to house the departments of Film, Graphics, Painting, and Photography. This will allow the College to consolidate the remainder of its departments close to those in the main building on Kensington Gore.

In this original proposal only the facade and front rooms of the Queensgate houses have been preserved with new building work behind up to and including the Jay Mews frontage. The deep site requires the incorporation of a toplit space to provide daylight to the center of the scheme, and this space divides the new Jay Mews building from the Queensgate building.

1 *Elevation to Jay Mews.*

1

2 *Section.*
3 *First and second floor plan.*

1 Jay mews
2 Entrance
3 Studio
4 Atrium and Galleries
5 Office
6 Ancillaries
7 Queens Gate

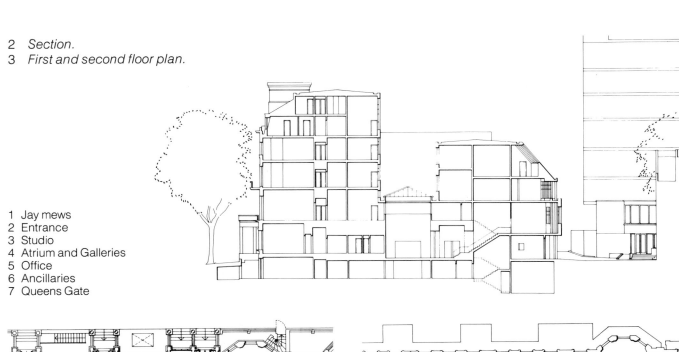

2

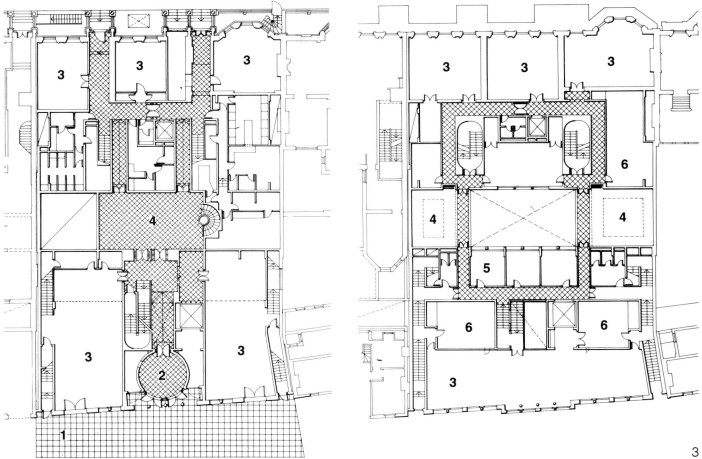

3

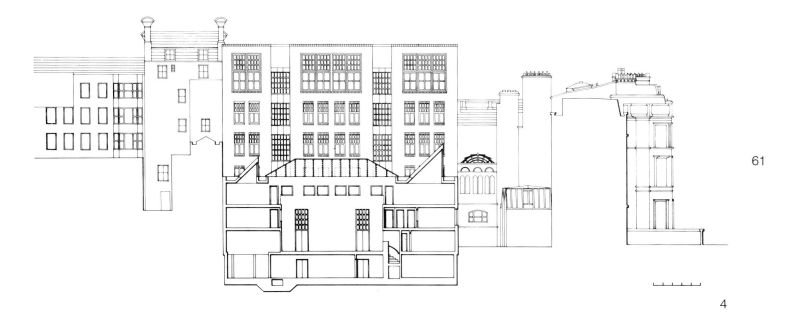

4

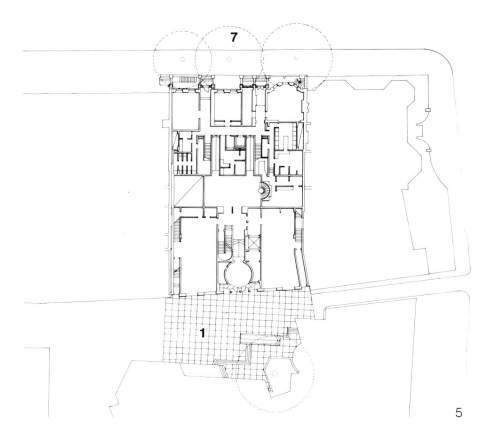

7

1

5

4 *Section.*
5 *Site plan.*

TWO COMMUNITY CENTERS

Melrose Avenue
Bletchley   1974

Welbourne Road
London   1976

62

These single story community buildings are located on urban sites and associated with residential precincts. The briefs were similar and called for flexible multi-purpose spaces suitable for a variety of recreational activities for different age groups.

In both buildings dry, pre-fabricated elements were used as far as possible.

At Melrose Avenue, a structure of nine tubular steel columns on a square grid supports an open-truss steel roof. External cladding is of glass-reinforced concrete. Exposed steel elements and doors are painted red, green, and yellow.

At Welbourne Road the structure is also of steel, but here the columns, consisting of I beams, are placed outside the external walls so as to leave the interior space unobstructed. The roof is spanned with solid steel beams. External cladding is of corrugated sheet steel with integral white plastic finish. External steel elements are painted white. To counteract a somewhat impoverished environment, there is an enclosed and protected courtyard within the curtilage of the building.

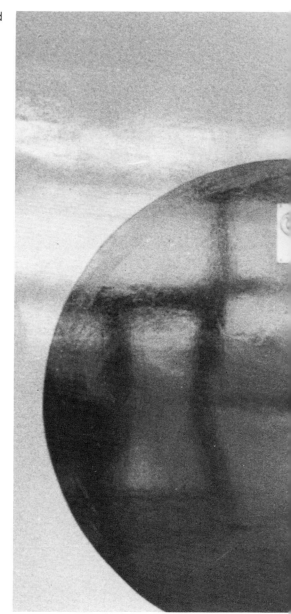

2 *Melrose Avenue.
  Axonometric.*
3 *Melrose Avenue.
  Exterior view.*

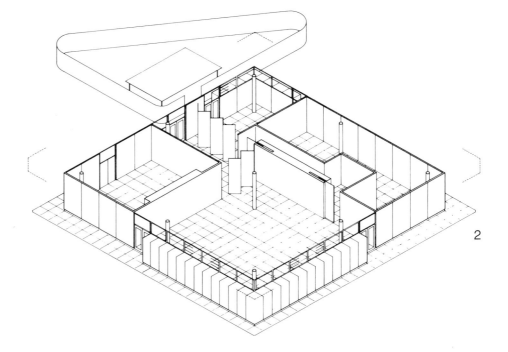

2

3

4   Melrose Centre.
    Detail of exterior.
5   Melrose Avenue.
    Axonometric.

4

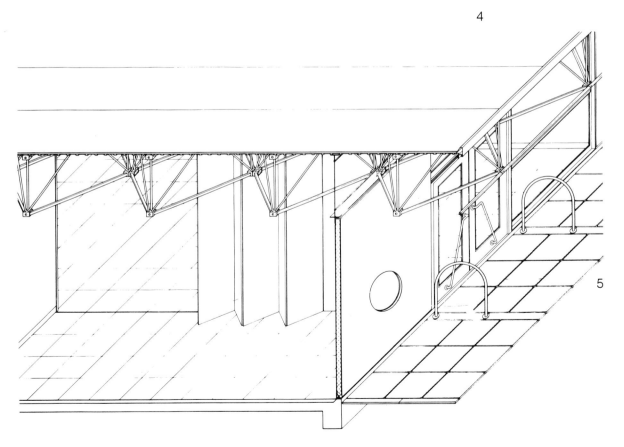

5

66

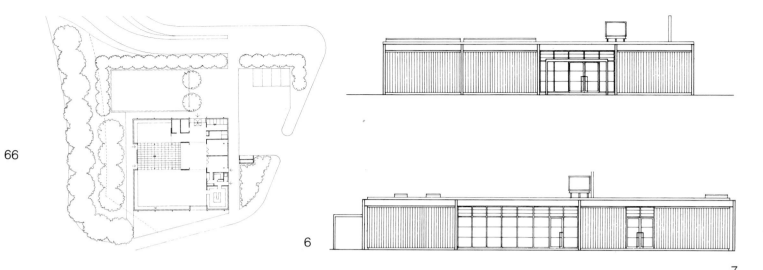

6

7

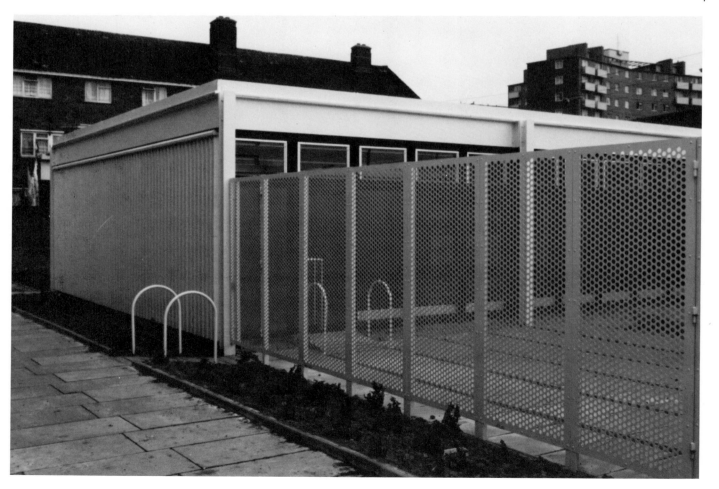

8

67

9

WEST GREEN ROAD

Old Persons Home
London   1976

68 This building occupies an awkward triangular site in a rather loosely structured urban context.

The program asked for accommodation for forty elderly people, divided into four "houses," each containing nine bed-sitting rooms and a common room. In addition, a large common room, a kitchen, bathrooms, administrative offices, and two managers' apartments were required.

Two wings of the building are arranged to create a forecourt. The large common room, which is combined with the entrance hall, overlooks this forecourt and the street beyond, and acts as the focal point of the building. The bed-sitting rooms and small common rooms look onto a private garden at the back.

The structure is of load-bearing brickwork, with red facings. The window frames are of anodized aluminum.

1 *Exterior view garden bed-sitting room windows.*
2 *Exterior view of entrance and main common room.*

1

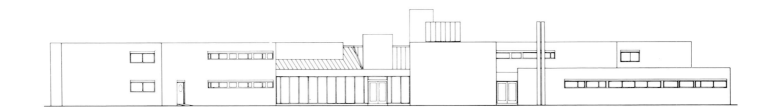

3

3 *Entrance elevation.*
4 *Exterior view from garden:*
   common room windows.
5 *Garden elevation.*
6 *Second floor plan.*
7 *First floor plan.*
8 *Axonometric from entrance side.*
9 *Axonometric from garden side.*

4

5

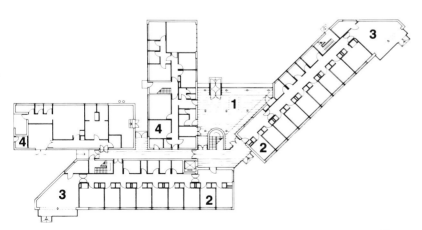

6

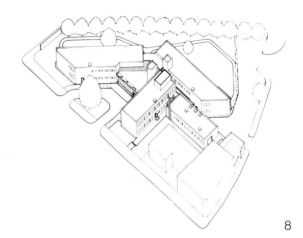

8

1 Entrance Hall   3 Common Room
2 Bedrooms   4 Administration and Service

7

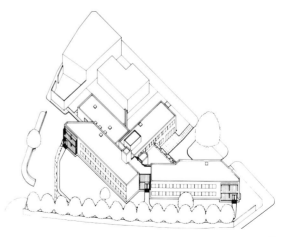

9

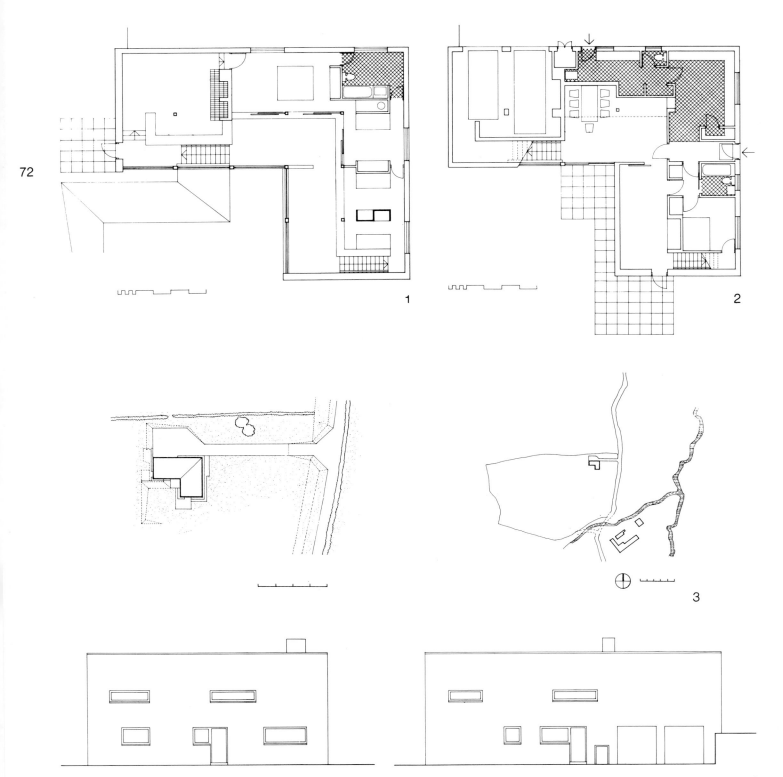

1

2

3

4

This small house, designed for a young farmer and his family, occupies an exposed site in a remote part of Wales.

The elements of the house—walls, openings, roof—are so composed as to convey the idea of shelter and vernacular simplicity. The organization of plan and section allows all the rooms to look onto a protected, south-facing courtyard. The hillside has been carved to protect this courtyard from the prevailing wind.

1 *First floor plan.*
2 *Second floor plan.*
3 *Site and location plans.*
4 *Entrance elevations.*
5 *Garden elevations.*
6 *Sections.*

73

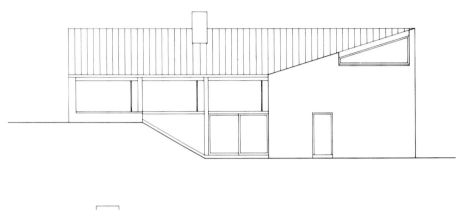

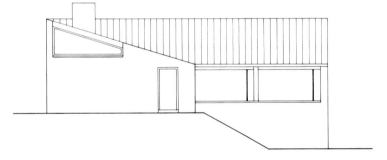

5

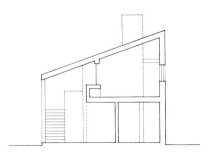

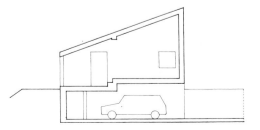

6

PILLWOOD 1

Cornwall   1975

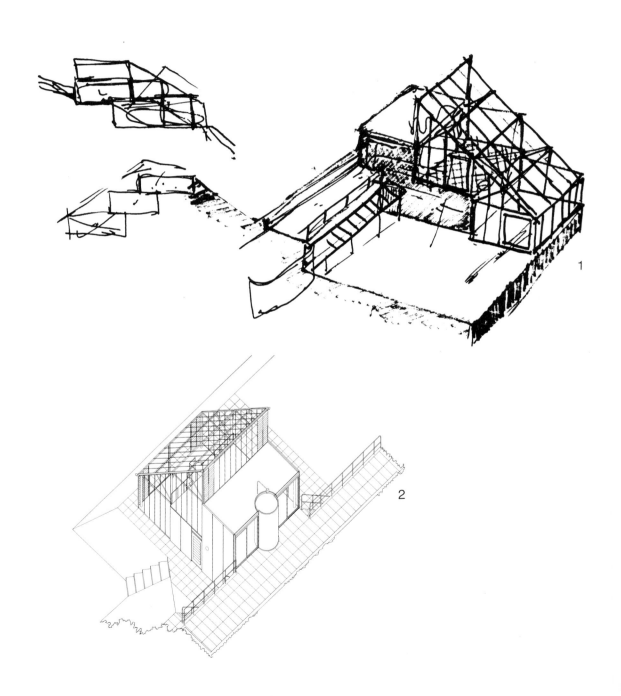

1

2

The house was designed for vacations, with a plan that could be modified to suit varying numbers of people. The site is one of outstanding natural beauty bordering on the estuary of the river Fal.

The structure consists of a tubular steel frame, with reinforced concrete floors. The external walls are of glass and G.R.P. polyurethane-filled panels, with neoprene joints. The steel frame is painted green, and the GRP panels are white. Background heating is provided by means of an underfloor hot water system.

1 *Preliminary sketches.*
2 *Axonometric.*
3 *Exterior detail.*

5　*Section.*
6　*Plan at lower level (garden).*
7　*Plan at upper level (entrance).*

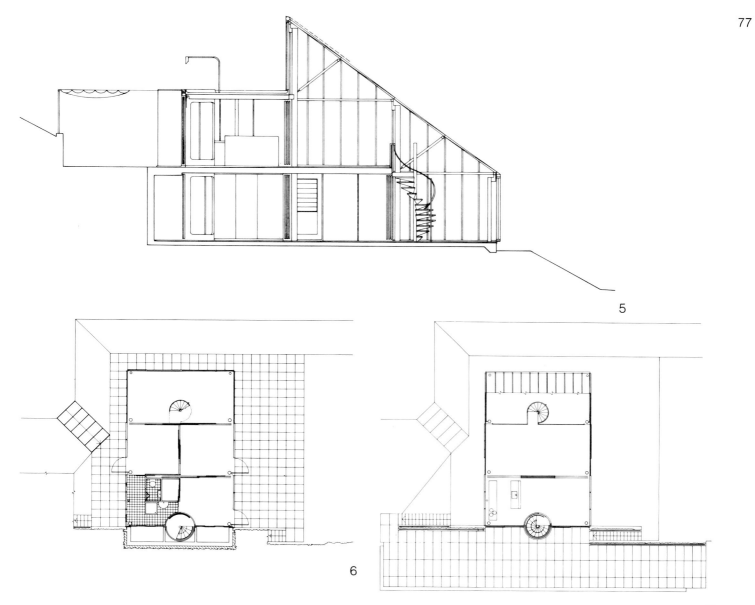

5

6

7

8 *View of bedroom.*
9 *Living room in summer.*
10 *Living room in winter.*

8

9

10

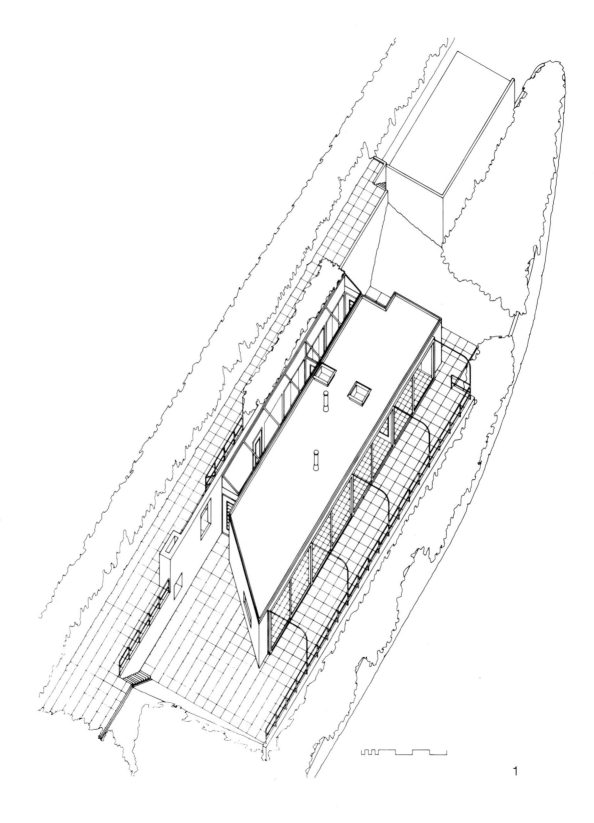

1

2

This house was planned for a graphics designer and his family on a site immediately adjacent to Pillwood 1.
The arrangement of the living/studio, kitchen, and bedrooms was introduced to allow the overall space to be used as one.
The house was to be placed at the top of a steep slope on a narrow site in such a way as to be invisible from the road behind, while at the same time enjoying the view of Pillcreek and the Fal estuary beyond.
Its construction technique was intended to be compatible with Pillwood 1.

1 *Axonometric.*
2 *View of model.*

3 *Preliminary sketches.*
4 *Plan.*

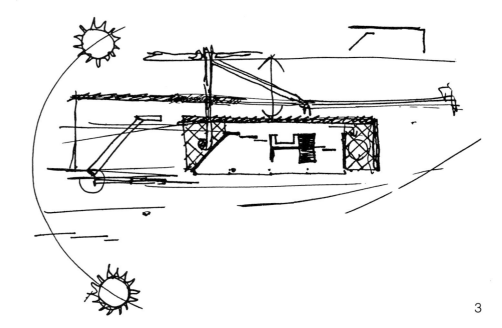

3

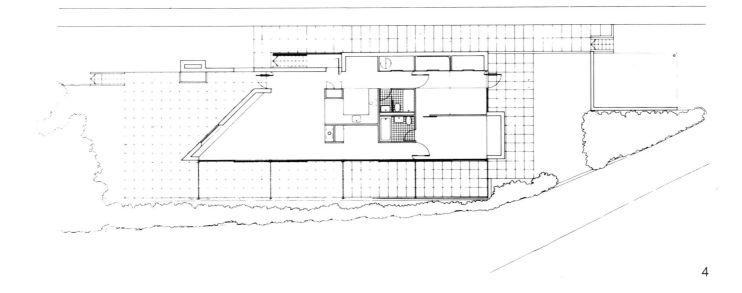

4

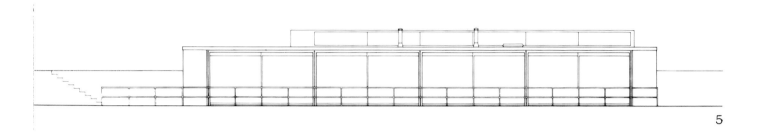

5

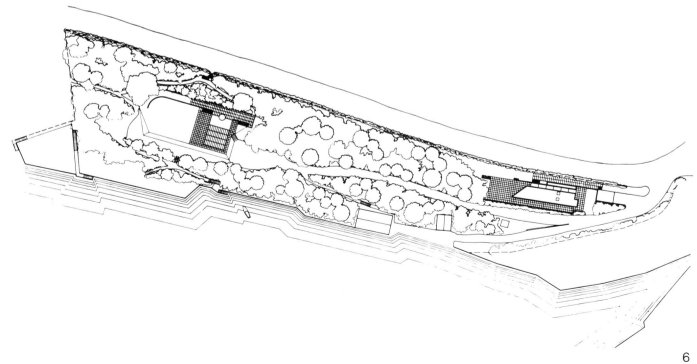

6

HOLIDAY CHALETS

Aviemore, Scotland   1973

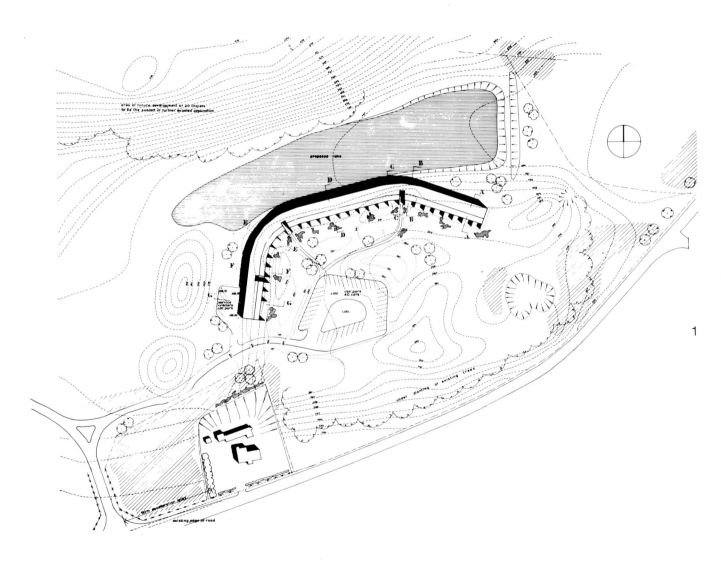

1

This group of 30 vacation units was designed for a site of exceptional natural beauty.
The form of the building was based on the natural contours of the site.
The project remained unbuilt.

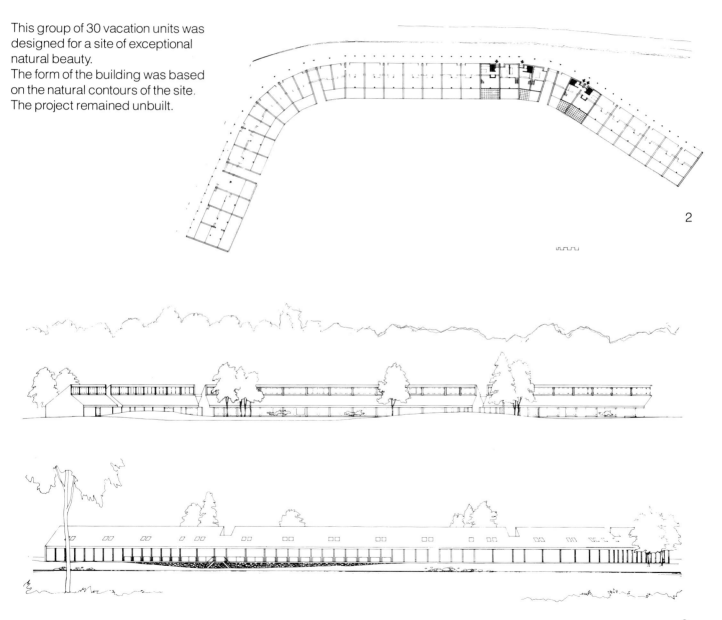

2

3

MILLBANK HOUSING

(Open Competition)   1976

86   This apartment project was to be
built on the Thames Embankment.
Our solution proposed that all the
apartments be accommodated in
three slender towers, so that the view
of the river from across the road
would be obstructed as little as
possible. The urban model was that
of a linear riverside park with isolated
buildings placed within it, contrasting
with the solidity of the city blocks
further inland.
The grouping creates the expecta-
tion of a fourth tower, but the space of
this tower is occupied by a void
acting as a common forecourt. In
order for the three towers to form a
finite group each tower has been
given a different geometrical shape.

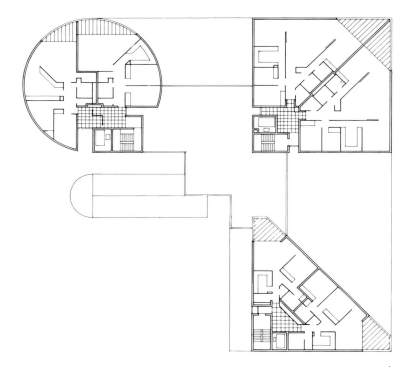

1

1 *First floor plan.*
2 *Site and first floor plan.*

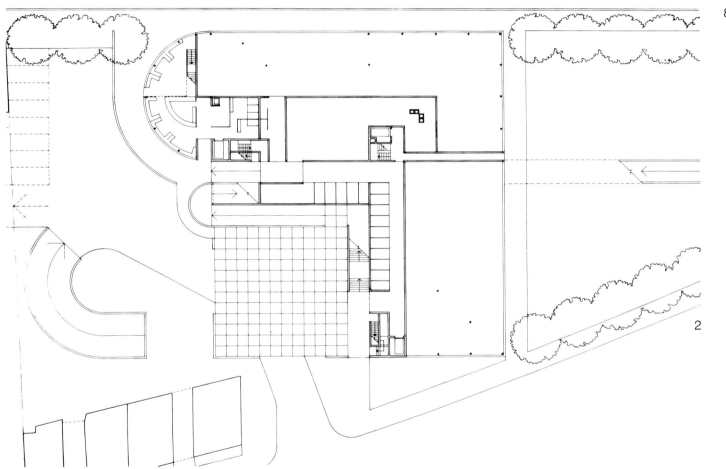

2

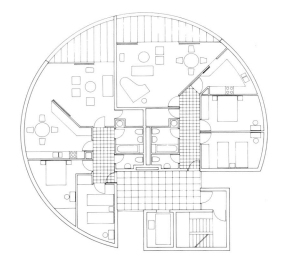

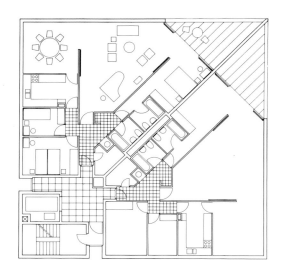

3

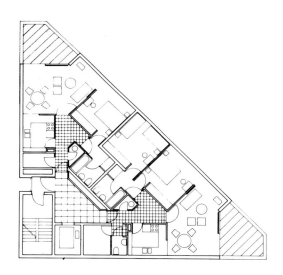

3 *Typical apartment plans.*
4 *Axonometric.*

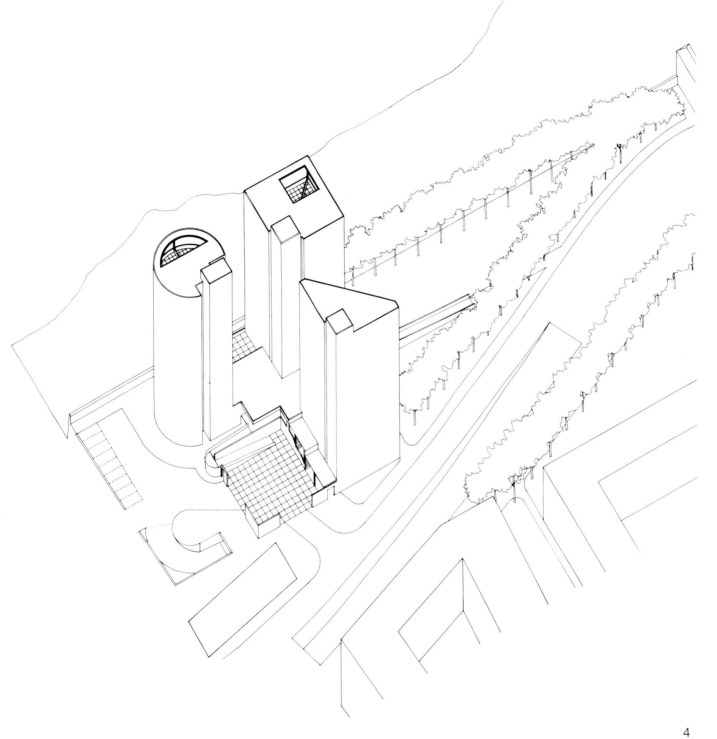

FENNY STRATFORD

(Corner Site)   1978

90   This project for infill housing is
     sited at the busy intersection of an
     old village, and the problem was
     to design a group of houses with
     small gardens that would reinforce
     the existing urban fabric while giving
     protection from the noise of traffic.
     Parking space is provided on site,
     and access to the houses is from the
     parking area.
     The houses are constructed of
     load-bearing brickwork with deep
     red facings. The roofs are of grey
     concrete tile.

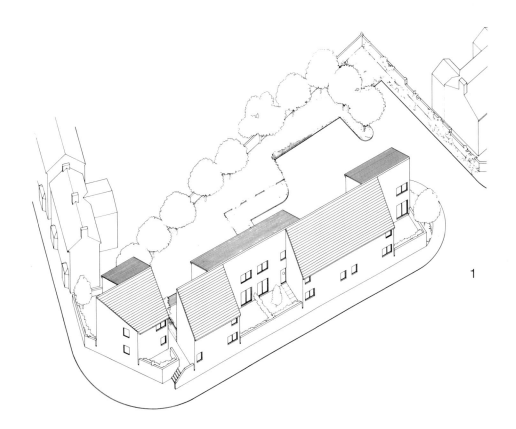

1

1   *Axonometric.*
2   *View from car park.*

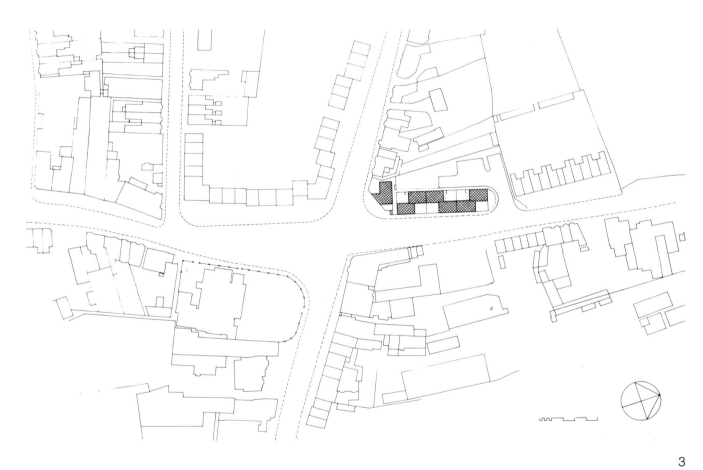

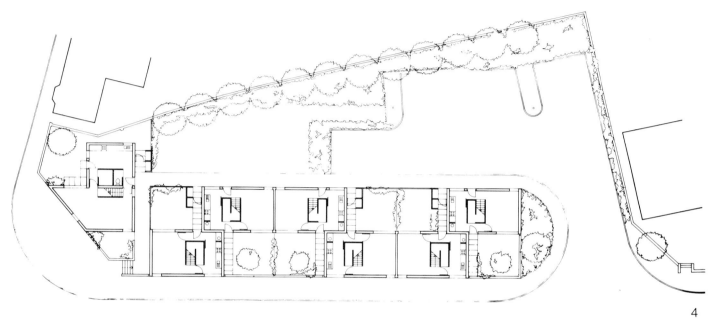

4

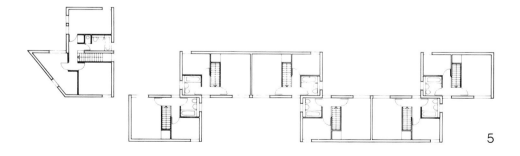

5

1 *Caversham Road.*
   Exterior view from street.
2 *Axonometric view*
   from Caversham Road.

1

CAVERSHAM ROAD AND GAISFORD STREET

London   1979

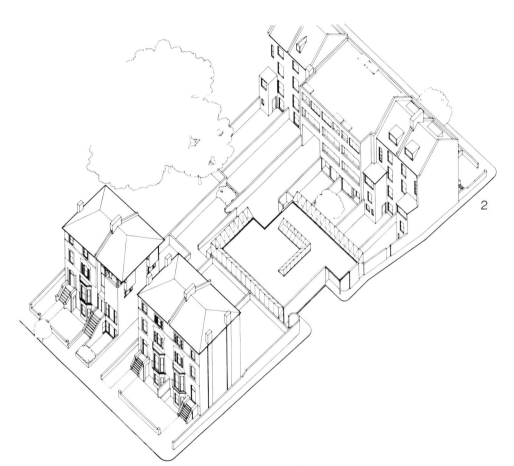

2

In this project, the problem was to fill gaps in two adjacent 19th- century residential streets.

On the Gaisford Street site, the space of three row houses was filled with five duplex apartments, all with direct access to the street. The public entrances are similar in form and scale to those in the existing row houses.

On the Caversham Road site, the missing half of a large semi-detached villa was replaced, to provide two new duplex apartments. The Italianate roof of the original villa has been extended over the new structure. The new fenestration has a contrasting pattern to that of the existing house, but agrees with it in scale.

In both buildings the lower apartments have access to private gardens, while the upper apartments have balconies.

The original brief called for a community center between the gardens of the new buildings, but this was later abandoned.

Both buildings are finished in stucco.

3

4

5

6

3 *Caversham Road. Upper Duplex Third floor.*
4 *Caversham Road. Upper Duplex Second floor.*
5 *Caversham Road. Lower Duplex First Floor.*

6 *Caversham Road. Lower Duplex Basement.*
7 *Caversham Road. Elevation.*
8 *Caversham Road. Exterior view from garden.*

7

8

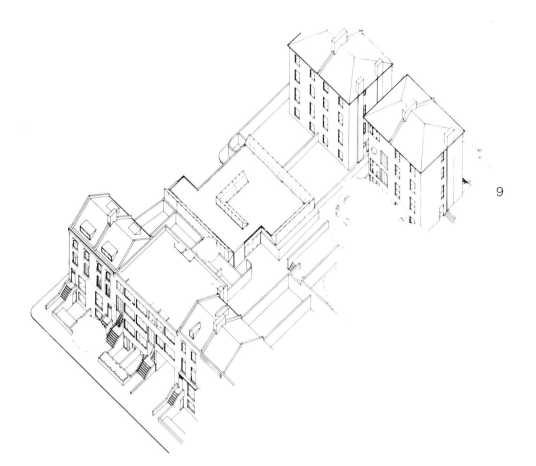

9   *Axonometric view
from Gaisford Street.*
10 *Gaisford Street.
Elevation.*

9

10

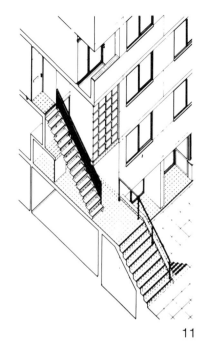

11

12

11 *Gaisford Street.*
   Axonometric detail.
12 *Gaisford Street.*
   Exterior view from street.

13 *Gaisford Street. Lower Duplex*
Second floor.

14 *Gaisford Street. Lower Duplex*
Third floor.

15 *Gaisford Street. Upper Duplex*
Basement.

16 *Gaisford Street. Upper Duplex*
First floor.

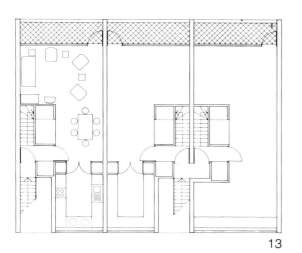

13

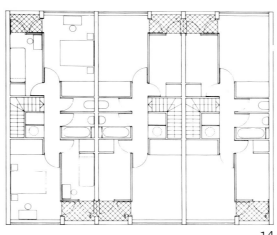

14

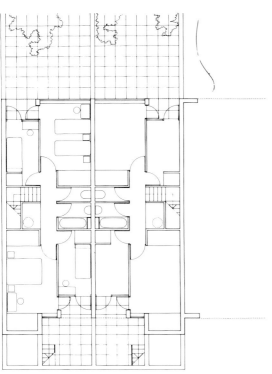

15

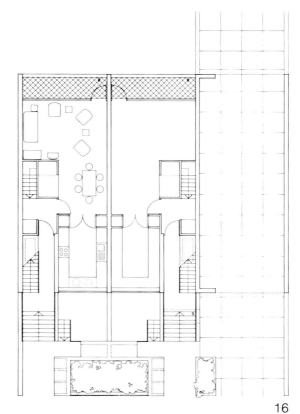

16

HORNSEY LANE

London   1980

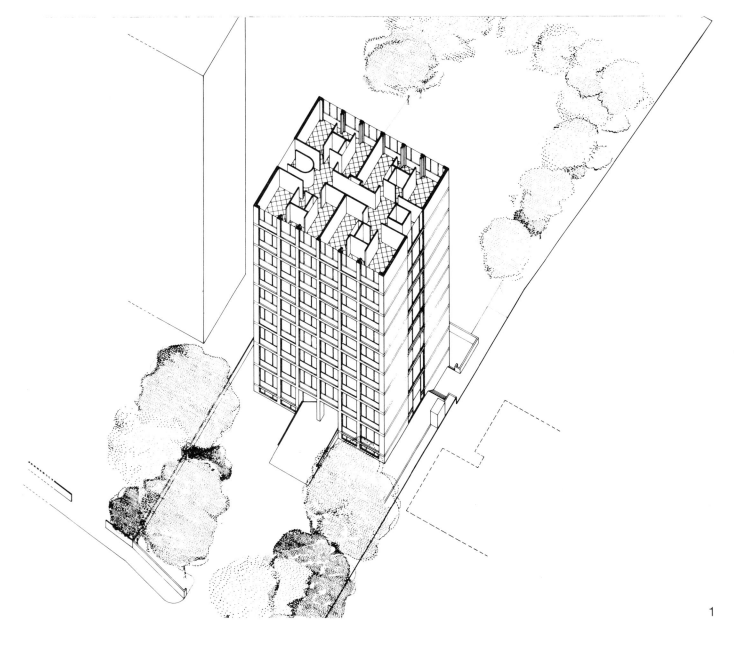

This building contains 34 two-person apartments, each consisting of two bed-sitting rooms, a kitchen and a bathroom. In addition the building contains a caretaker's apartment, a common room and a laundry.

The street in which the building is located was originally lined with substantial villas set back from the road, which have been progressively replaced by small apartment blocks. The building is constructed of load-bearing brickwork with red facings. The floors are of insitu reinforced concrete.

101

2

3 *Typical floor plan.*
4 *First floor plan.*

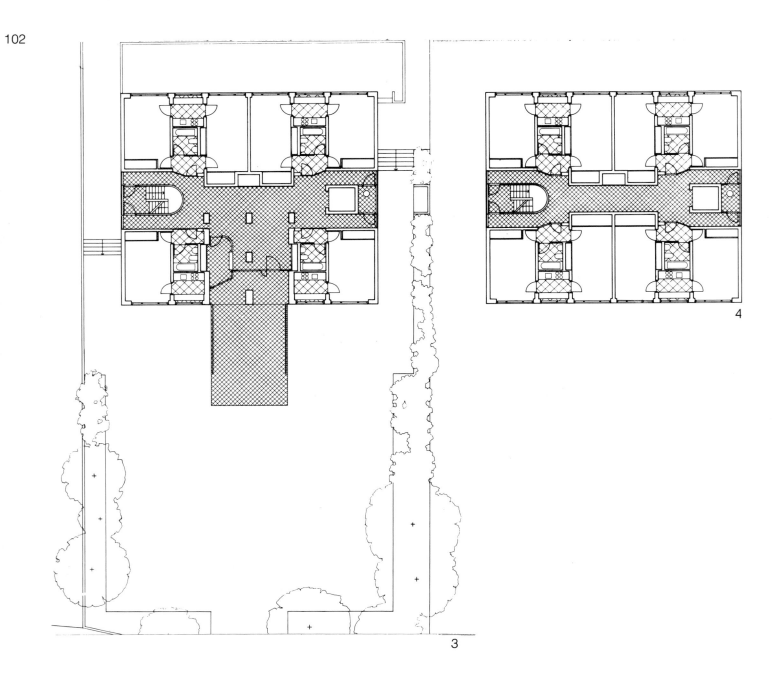

3

4

5

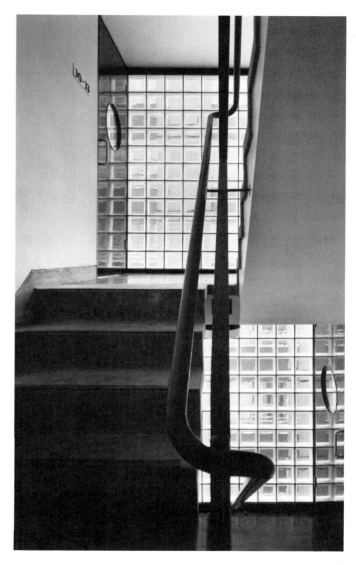

6

The program called for 152 dwellings for families of two to seven people, the majority of which should consist of houses with integral garages. The layout attempted to create an urban scale by stressing the street as the locus of the *res publica* and contrasting this to the *res privata* of gardens and childrens' play spaces. The scheme illustrates the difficulty of establishing an urban environment within a context that is fundamentally suburban in concept. Our preference was for three story terraces, but the client preferred two stories, and the resultant layout is a compromise between the two.

In the street facade, the bays containing garages, living rooms, and loggias are projected forward to emphasize the individuality of each house within the overall discipline of the terrace.
The scheme is constructed in load-bearing brickwork with buff-colored facings and string courses, sills and lintels of darker brick. The roofs are of concrete tiles and the doors and window frames are of dark stained wood. The materials were largely determined by the client, and we only had a limited control over colors and finishes.

1 *Three-story row houses. Exterior view from street.*
2 *Two-story row houses. Exterior view from street.*

105

2

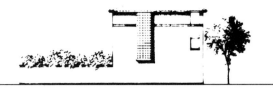
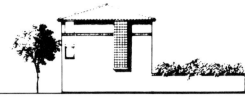

3

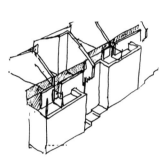

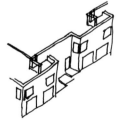

4

3 *Elevation to feeder road.*
4 *Three-story row houses.*
   Exterior view of end.
5 *Study sketches.*
6 *Site plan.*
7 *Elevation to*
   three-story row houses.

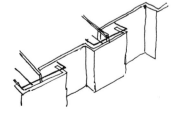

5

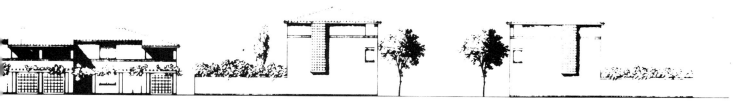

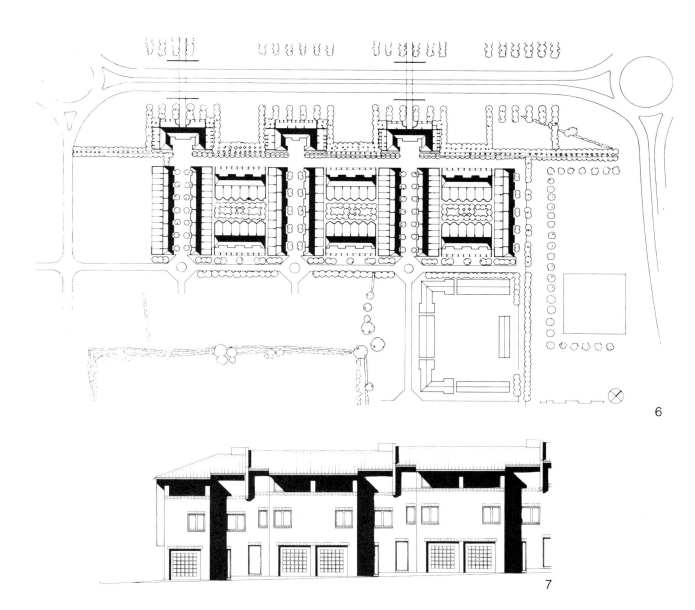

6

7

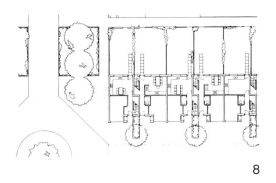

8

11

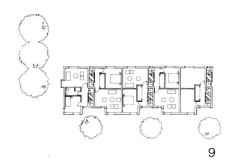

9

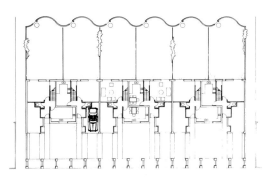

12

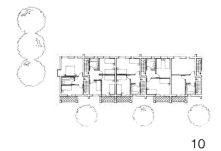

10

8 Three-story row houses.
   Ground floor plan.
9 Three-story row houses.
   Second floor plan.
10 Three-story row houses.
   Third floor plan.
11 Two-story row houses.
   Second floor plan.
12 Two-story row houses.
   First floor plan.
13 Two-story court building.
   First floor plan.
14 Two-story court building.
   Second floor plan.
15 Exterior view
   of court building.

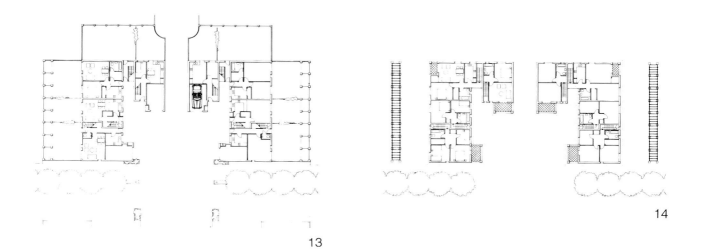

13

14

15

SHRUBLAND ROAD AND ALBION DRIVE

London   1984

110   This project consists of infill housing
on three separate sites of a residential quarter dating from the 1840s.
The quarter has a strong architectural character, consisting of semidetached neo-classical buildings.
In our solution, the existing typology
has been used and adapted to
modern requirements. The existing
frontage lines, number of stories,
entrance systems, window types,
and materials have been repeated.
In terms of architectural language,
the facade of each semi-detached
unit has a gable pediment, which is
similar to one of the original types to
be found in the quarter. The entrance
doors are in a recessed porch. This
porch has a central column which
marks the line of the party wall. The
houses are uniform in their external

1

1   *External view
    of street facade.*
2   *External view
    of street facades.*

2

3

appearance, concealing a variety of house and apartment types within. An important aim of the project was to reinforce the existing architecture and assert the street frontage as the principle facade, thus emphasizing the street as a place of public appearance. This contrasts with many recent housing schemes which turn their backs on the street, and contribute to the destruction of the public realm.

The houses are constructed of load-bearing brickwork with London stock facings to match the existing houses. The ground floors have stucco rustication. The roofs are of slate and windows are of wood painted white. Copings and sills are of reconstructed bath stone.

4

3 *Typical local house facade.*
4 *Typical local house facades.*

5

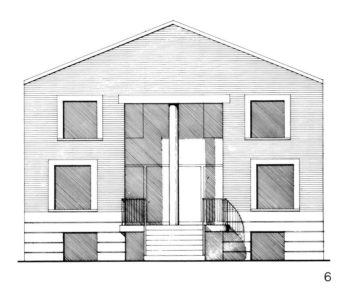

6

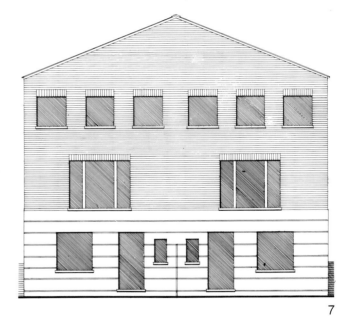

7

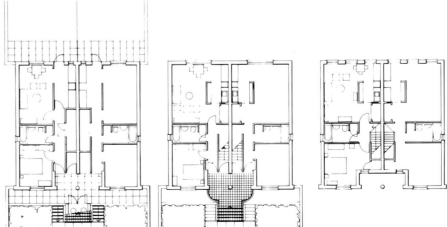

5 *Street elevations.*
6 *Street elevation.*
7 *Garden elevation.*
8 *Floor plans of two-person apartments.*

8

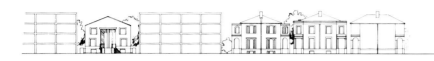

9

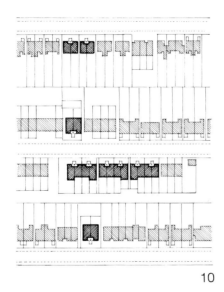

10

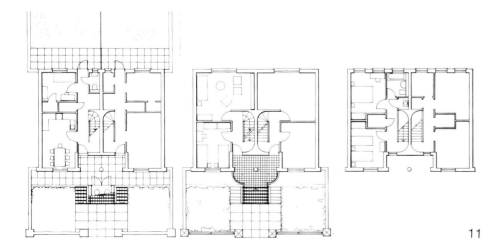

11

9   *Street elevations.*
10 *Site plan.*
11 *Floor plans*
     of seven-person houses.

CHURCH CRESCENT

London   1984

114   This project consists of four houses
on a wedge-shaped site adjacent to
a church and churchyard. The
immediate urban context is very
fragmented. The shape of the site
suggested a solution in terms of
isolated, pavilion-like buildings.
The solution adopted is based on the
traditional English typology of the
semi-detached villa. Each villa
contains two three-story, eight-
person houses, which are entered
from the sides. The buildings consist
of traditional tectonic elements such
as hipped roof, punched windows,
bow windows, and loggias. But,
because of the heterogeneous
character of the site, these have
been treated with great freedom
from the point of view of architectural
language.
The construction is of load-bearing
concrete blocks, finished in stucco
above a brick plinth. Window frames
are of powder-coated aluminum. The
roof is of concrete tile.

1   *Exterior view*
    of entrance facade.
2   *Exterior facade detail.*

1

3

3   Street elevation.
4   Site plan.
5   Side elevation.
6   Garden elevation.
7   Exterior view from street.
8   L-R: First, Second
    and Third floor plans.

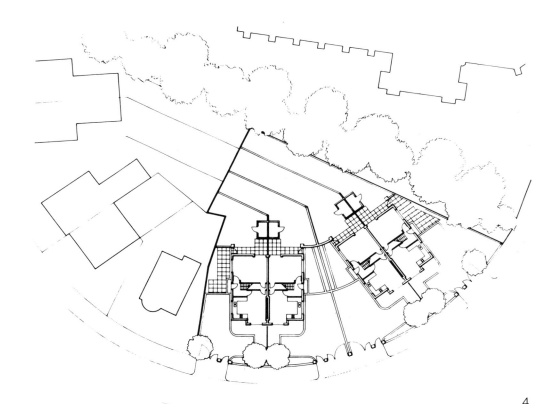

4

5

6

7

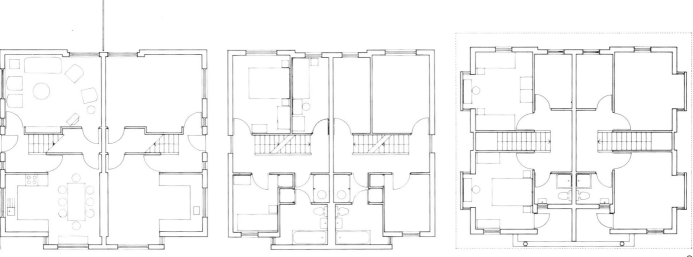

8

TWO MILE ASH

Milton Keynes   1984

118

1

2

3

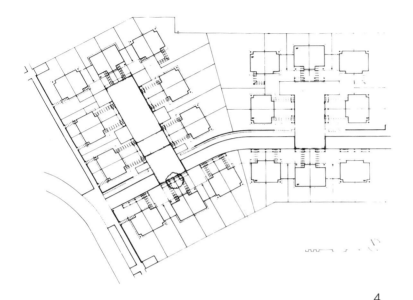

4

This project consists of 54 houses for families of two to five people.
Whereas Oldbrook 2 consisted of fully subsidized houses for rent, in this project the houses were for sale and the consequent need for adaptation to market forces accounts for the clients preference for semi-detached units.
An additional symptom of "privatization" is the fact that the constructional system was left to the builder. The houses are constructed of wood frame with brick facings.
The roofs are of concrete tile, and the doors and window frames are of dark stained wood.

1   *Exterior view from street.*
2   *Elevation.*
3   *Typical floor plans.*
4   *Site plan.*
5   *Exterior view from street.*

WILLEN PARK

Milton Keynes   1984

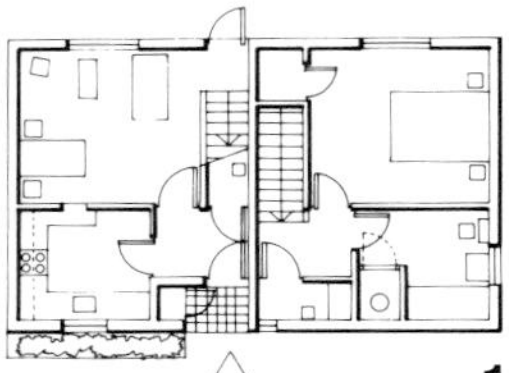

1

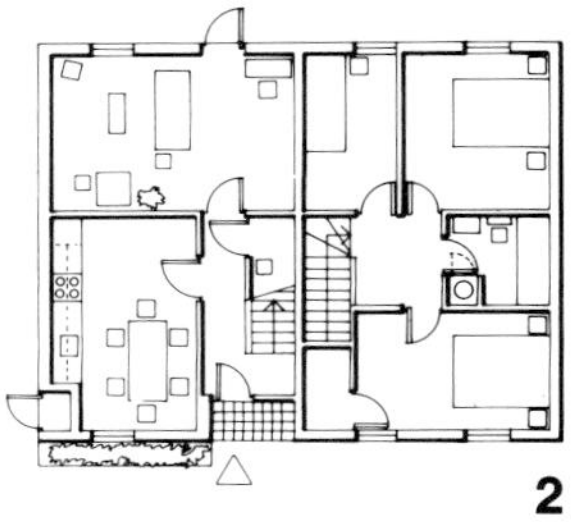

2

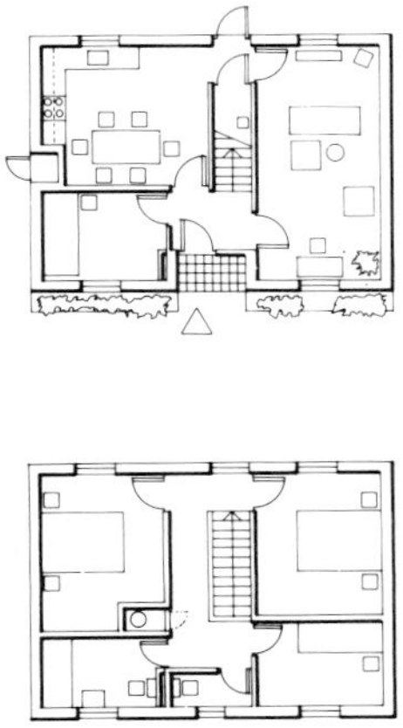

3

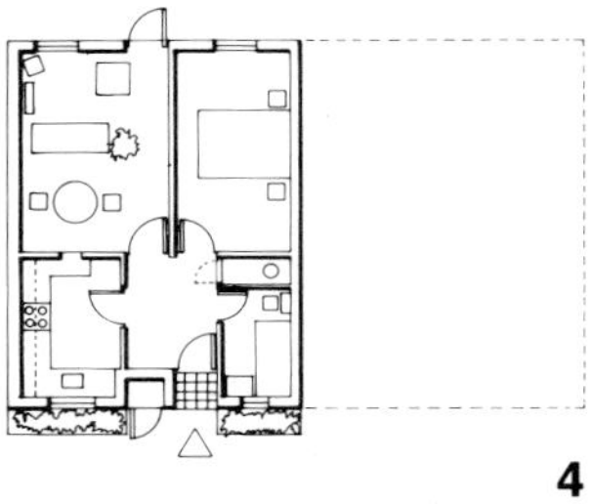

4

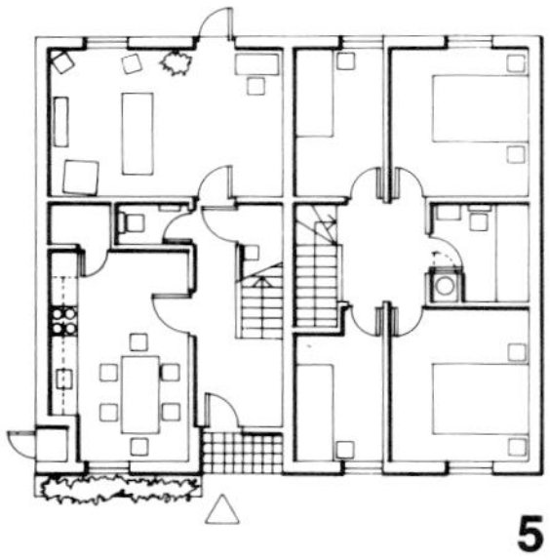

5

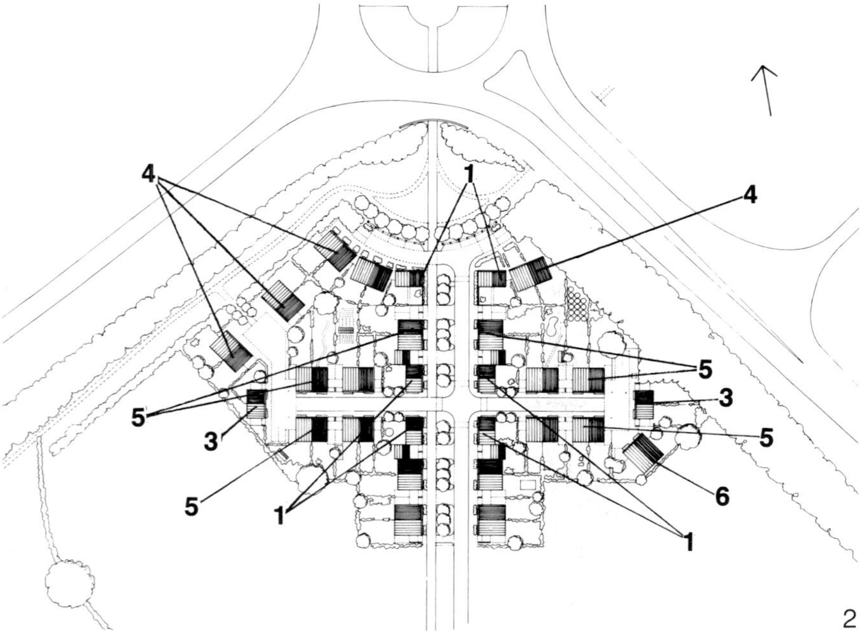

6

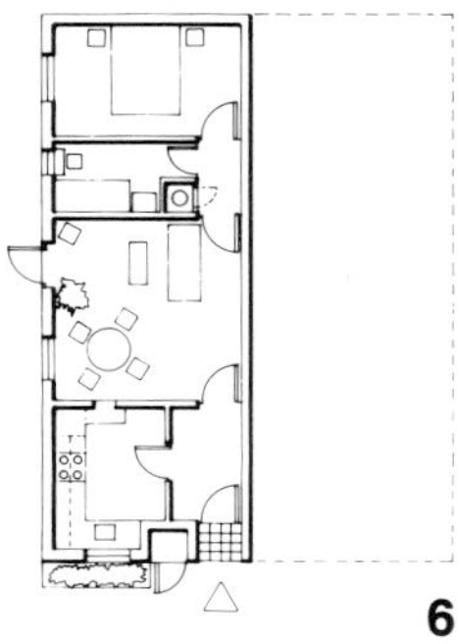

2

This project consists of 48 houses for families of two to six people.
The program and method of construction were similar to those of Two Mile Ash.
The site plan was severely constrained by the pre-existing alignment of pedestrian and vehicle roads, which were focused onto a major traffic roundabout.

3

1   *Plans of house types.*
2   *Site plan.*
3   *Axonometric.*
4   *Exterior view.*

4

IBA HOUSING COMPETITION

Berlin   1987

122   This project for the Internationale Bauausstellung (IBA) was the subject of a limited international competition. The program called for a mixed development including public housing with communal gardens and Kindergarten, commercial offices, a printing works, and various specialized functions such as a street cleaning depot, type repair workshops, and a multi-story car park. The site locations of the housing, offices, and printing works were prescribed in the program by the organizers.

The site, which is close to the Tiergarten, is made up of two urban blocks divided by Lutzowstrasse and bounded by Karlsbad, Flotwellstrasse and Pohlstrasse. There are many existing buildings which have to be retained and integrated with the new work. Lutzowstrasse, which is the armature of the site, has been terminated in a new platz where it joins Flotwellstrasse. This has been lined with shops and complements Lutzowplatz at its westerly end.

New public housing lines Pohlstrasse and Karlsbad; commercial offices line Flotwellstrasse, and Lutzowstrasse has a mix of both functions. These have been inserted between existing buildings.

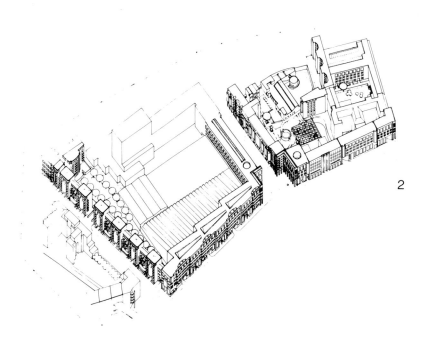

2

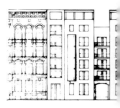

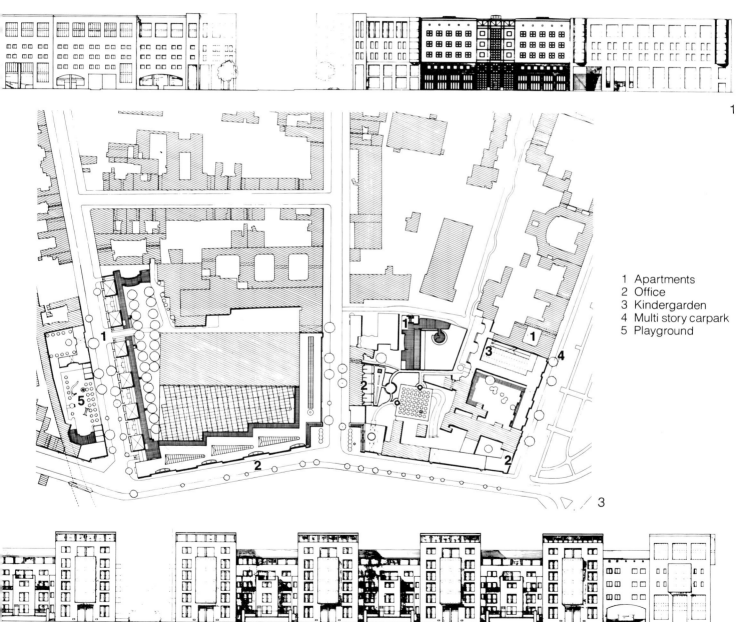

1

123

1 Apartments
2 Office
3 Kindergarden
4 Multi story carpark
5 Playground

3

4

PRINT AND MAP SHOP

Weinreb & Douwma
London   1969

124 This project involved the conversion of two existing shops into a showroom for prints. Advantage was taken of the high ceilings to provide a mezzanine level, with storage for portfolios underneath.

The clients' program called for extensive built-in and freestanding cabinets for the storage and display of prints, and for a permanent, but changing, exhibition of prints and maps on the walls.

The cabinets are of steamed birch, with chromium-plated steel hardware. The walls are lined with untreated flooring cork. The floor has a dark brown carpet.

1

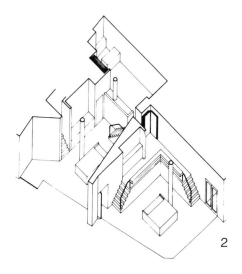

2

3

1 *Interior view.*
2 *Axonometric.*
3 *Interior view.*

DADA AND SURREALIST EXHIBITION

Hayward Gallery
London   1978

The exhibition consisted of seven-
teen sections taking their titles from
Dada and Surrealist magazines.
Each section was entered through an
introductory space in the form of a
half cylinder, on which graphic
material from the relevant magazine
was mounted.

1

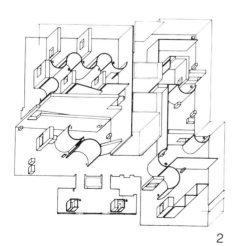

2

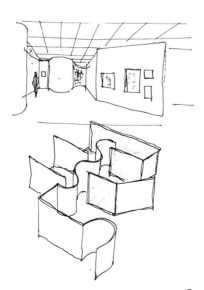

3

1 *View of exhibition.*
2 *Axonometric.*
3 *Study sketches.*

THE ARTS OF BENGAL EXHIBITION

Whitechapel Art Gallery
London   1979

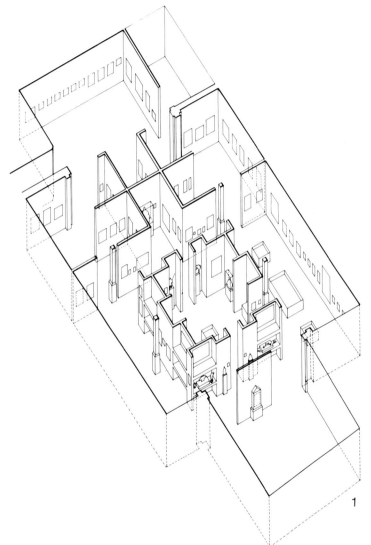

1

2

The exhibition contained examples of the whole range of religious and secular art of Bengal from the 12th century to the 20th century. The low-budget installation was restricted to the panels, light fittings and fixtures already belonging to the gallery.

Two kinds of space were created; a central "shrine," analogous to a temple, for the display of medieval religious sculpture, and a "ambulatory" containing secular paintings and craft work arranged chronologically.

1 *Axonometric.*
2 *View of "shrine."*

Hayward Gallery
London   1981

The installation consisted of large spaces punctuated by angled screens or small "rooms." The sculpture was displayed on free-standing plinths, and the smaller three dimensional objects were arranged on low shelves integral with the wall surfaces.

The color on the display surfaces, which varied from room to room, was chosen to emphasize the characteristics of each period of Picasso's work.

1   *View of exhibition.*   127

1

SIR CHRISTOPHER WREN EXHIBITION

Whitechapel Art Gallery
London   1982

128   This exhibition of architectural
drawings and models consisted of a
series of rooms connected, in enfi-
lade, by means of a "collection"
of Baroque doorways based on
Wren's designs.
The doorways were more strongly
lit than the surrounding walls and
ceiling, and marked the circulation
route through the exhibition, some-
times "framing" the exhibits.

1   *View of exhibition.*
2   *Axonometric.*
3   *Study sketches.*

1

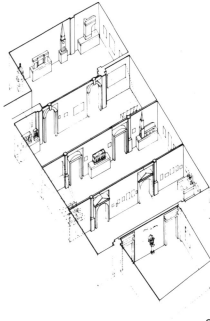

2

3

This traveling exhibition was designed to exhibit the furniture and
architecture of Adolf Loos.
It was made of prefabricated sections which, when assembled,
defined a series of rhythmically
linked volumes based on the geom-
etry of the cube. The treatment of
walls and ceilings refers obliquely to
themes in Loos's houses, but care
has been taken to create a background to the exhibits which is
unassertive.

129

1   *View of exhibition*
2   *Study sketches.*
3   *Axonometric.*

1

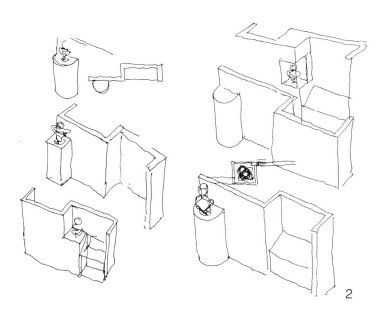

2

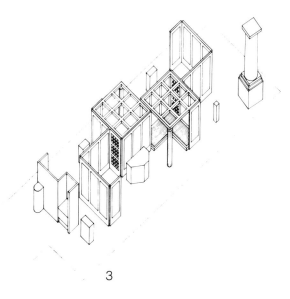

3

WHITECHAPEL ART GALLERY

Extensions and Refurbishment
London   1985

130   This project consists of alterations
and additions to the Whitechapel
Art Gallery, designed by Harrison
Townsend in 1898 and built
in 1901.

The original intention of the founders
was to make art available to the poor
of east London, and the Gallery
continues to play an important role in
the local (predominantly immigrant)
community. Since the war the Gallery
has also developed an international
reputation as a venue for the exhibition of modern art. The purpose of
the alterations was to enhance and
develop both these uses, and this
entailed the following work:

1. The upgrading of the environment
   of the existing galleries by the
   installation of air conditioning, u.v.
   and sunlight control, new artificial
   lighting, and a security system.
2. The provision of a new small
   gallery.
3. The replacement of the public
   staircases to make a more visible
   connection between the two floors
   and to facilitate the independent
   use of the first and second floor
   galleries.

1   *Original drawing of facade with
    Walter Crane's mural
    superimposed.*
2   *Exterior view of facade from
    Angel Alley.*

·WHITECHAPEL ART GALLERY·
IN COURSE OF ERECTION AT THE EXPENSE OF
HARRISON TOWNSEND ARCHT.   MR J. PASSMORE EDWARDS

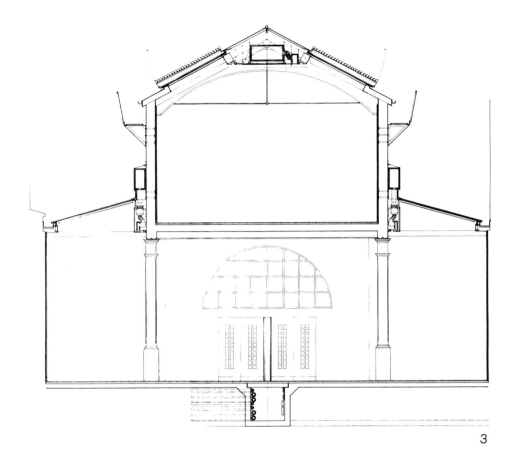

3

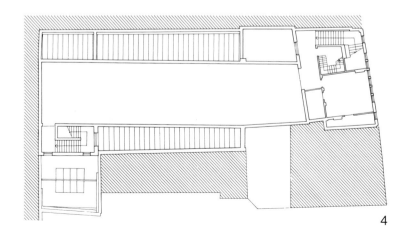

4

3 Section.
4 Original building.
Second floor plan.

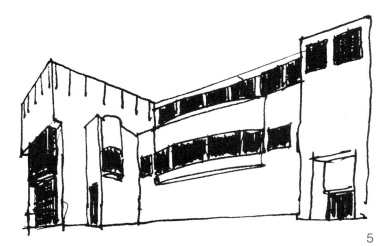

5 *Study sketch.*
6 *Exterior view
of facade showing context.*

5

6

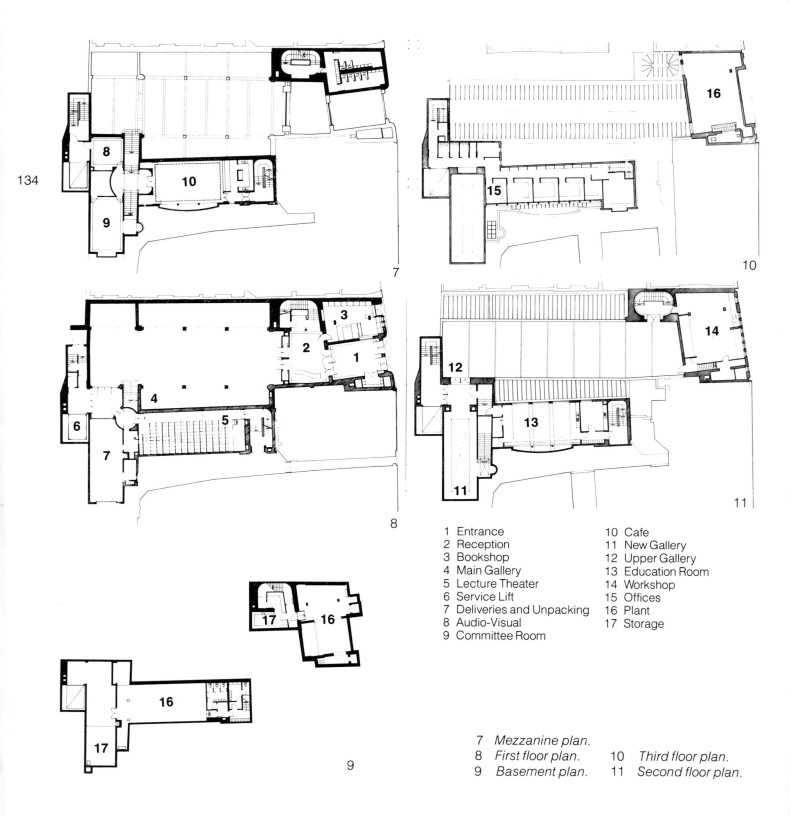

134

7

10

8

11

1 Entrance
2 Reception
3 Bookshop
4 Main Gallery
5 Lecture Theater
6 Service Lift
7 Deliveries and Unpacking
8 Audio-Visual
9 Committee Room

10 Cafe
11 New Gallery
12 Upper Gallery
13 Education Room
14 Workshop
15 Offices
16 Plant
17 Storage

9

7 Mezzanine plan.
8 First floor plan.
9 Basement plan.
10 Third floor plan.
11 Second floor plan.

4. The provision of new or improved ancillary accommodation for the public, including a lecture theater, studio, bookshop, restaurant, and cloakrooms.
5. The provision of new support facilities including offices, storage space, workshop, and freight elevator.

The building is listed as Grade II and the modifications were conditional on the preservation of the facade to Whitechapel High Street and the conservation of the main gallery spaces in their original form. Most of the modifications concerned the secondary accommodation and the only changes affecting the galleries were to the public stairs. These have been carried out in such a way that the integrity of the two original gallery spaces has been preserved.

The new accommodation was provided both within the envelope of the existing building and in a new extension occupying a narrow strip of land in Angel Alley previously occupied by a 19th-century school building. The new elements both internally and externally have been designed in a way that is sympathetic to the existing fabric, without imitating it.

12 *View of staircase in reception lobby.*
13 *View of upper gallery.*

12

13

14 *View of reception lobby*
   from lower gallery.
15 *View of cafe.*
16 *Cut-away axonometric.*

The internal finishes are: walls and ceilings, painted white; doors, painted or stained wood; gallery floors, maple strip; staircases and lobby floors, terrazzo; handrails and hardware, stainless steel. The external finishes are: walls, light buff facing bricks with darker brick string courses; windows, aluminum and steel.

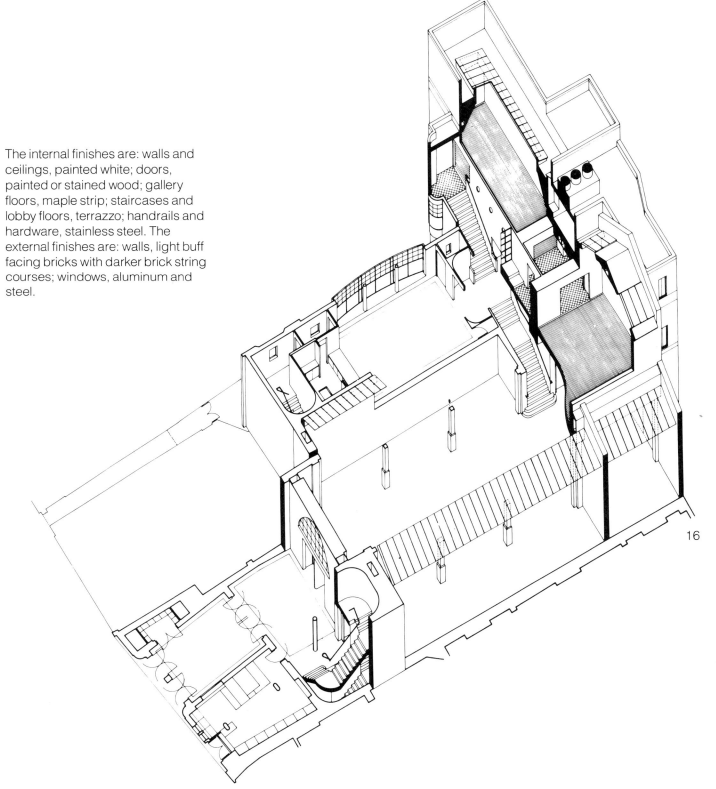

16

1 *Exterior view from Pall Mall East.*
2 *Exterior view from portico of National Gallery.*

VIEW FROM PALL MALL EAST

The program for this competition called for a new building to be linked to the Wilkin's building by a bridge over a public footpath. The top floor of this new building was to form an extension of the existing galleries, while the lower floors were to contain an entrance foyer, bookshop, changing exhibition space, restau-rant, lecture theater, and trustees' offices, as well as a loading bay and storage.

In our solution the new structure is treated both as an extension and as a building in its own right, approximating to an urban typology exemplified by the many clubs in the vicinity. The plan is organized symmetrically about a grand staircase leading from entrance foyer to gallery level in a single flight. An inflection of the extension towards the southeast was avoided as compromising the self-sufficiency of the Wilkin's facade and weakening the northwest corner of Trafalgar Square.

139

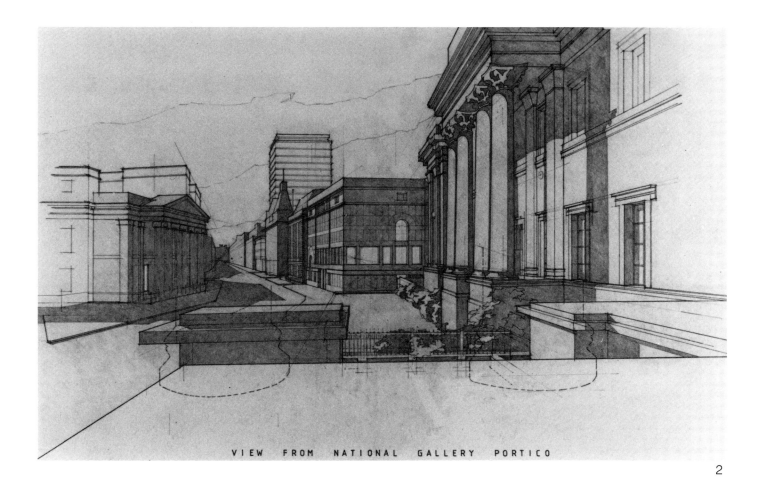

VIEW FROM NATIONAL GALLERY PORTICO

140

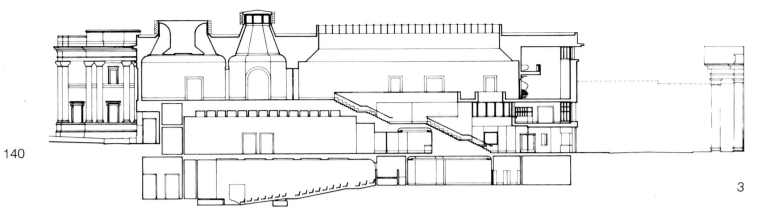

3

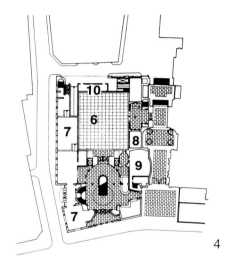

4

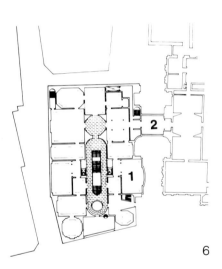

6

1 Galleries
2 Bridge Connection
3 Cafe/Restaurant
4 Trustees
5 Administration
6 Exhibition Hall
7 Shop
8 Coats
9 Audio-Visual
10 Service/Stores
11 Plant

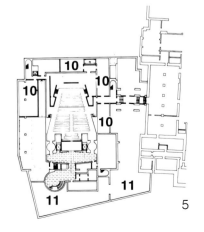

5

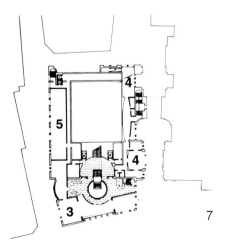

7

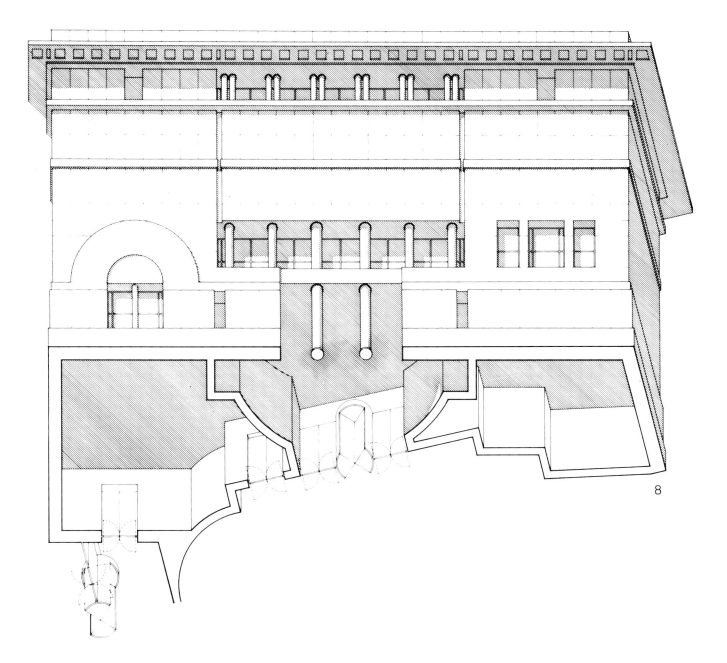

8

3 Section.
4 First floor plan.
5 Basement plan.
6 Second floor plan.
7 Mezzanine plan.
8 Axonometric of main facade.

STAEDEL INSTITUTE OF ART

Frankfurt (Limited Competition, Second Prize)   1986

142 The original neo-Renaissance wing
of the Staedel Institute of Art was built
in 1870. It was extended in the early
20th century to form an H-shaped
building.
The site of the extension was at right
angles to the river along Holbeinstrasse between the old gallery
and the Staedelschule, closing off
one side of the existing sculpture
garden.
The program asked for a new permanent gallery on the second floor,
connected by a bridge to the main
gallery floor of the old building, and a
changing exhibition space on the
ground floor. In addition, cabinetti,
offices, storage space with loading
bay, and a lecture theater were
required.

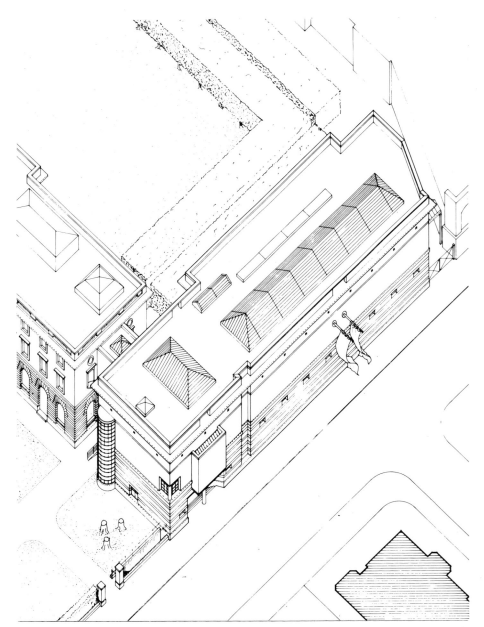

1 *Axonometric
    from Holbeinstrasse.*
2 *Elevation to Holbeinstrasse.*
3 *Axonometric
    from sculpture garden.*

1

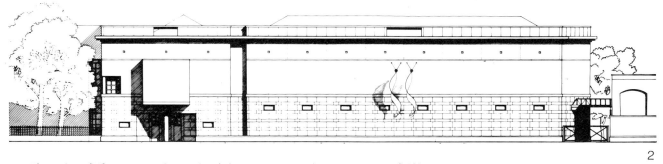

2

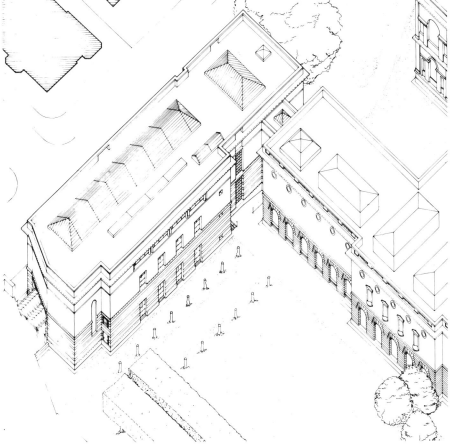

3

The scheme is expressed as a separate self-contained building, which is articulated into bays relating to axes generated from the existing site configuration. The character of the gallery spaces relates to their use, with top-lit permanent galleries and cabinetti, and an artificially lit, more flexible space for the changing exhibitions at ground floor level.

The internal public circulation is organized to relate to the garden and allows the galleries to be run separately, or as self-contained elements.

The materials and architectural motifs make reference to the existing building, comprising a sandstone base, rendered facades with stone cornice, and parapet.

144

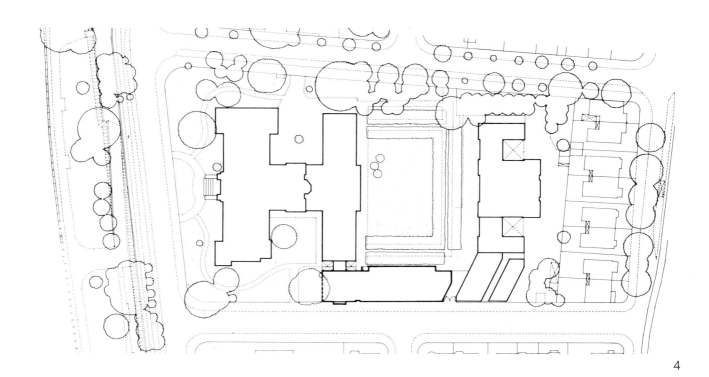

4

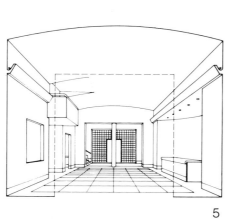

5

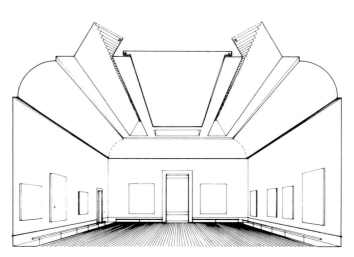

6

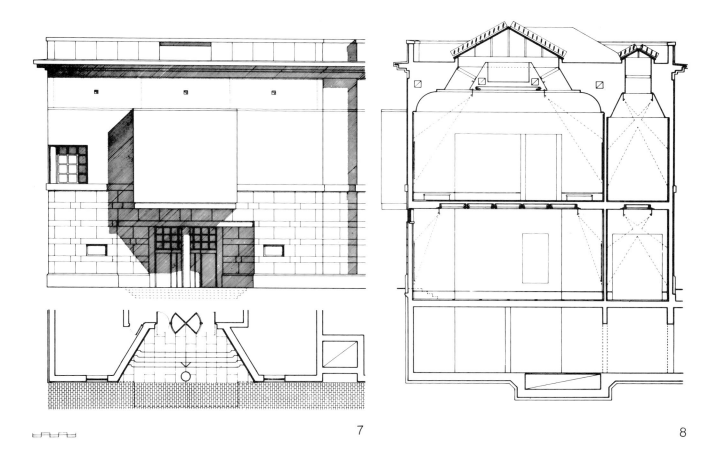

7

8

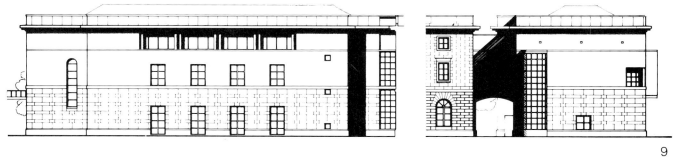

9

146

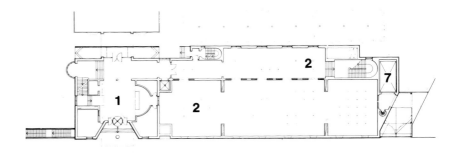

10

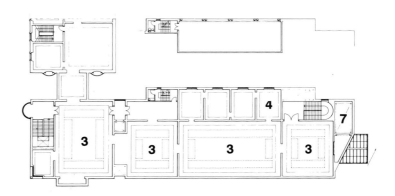

11

1 Entrance   5 Services/Storage/Plant
2 Exhibition   6 Lecture Theater
3 Gallery   7 Service
4 Cabinet

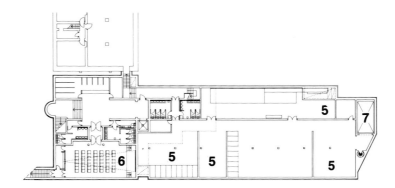

12

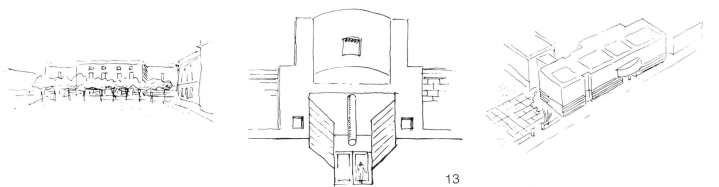

13

14

1 *Site plan.*
2 *Axonometric showing
main circulation.*

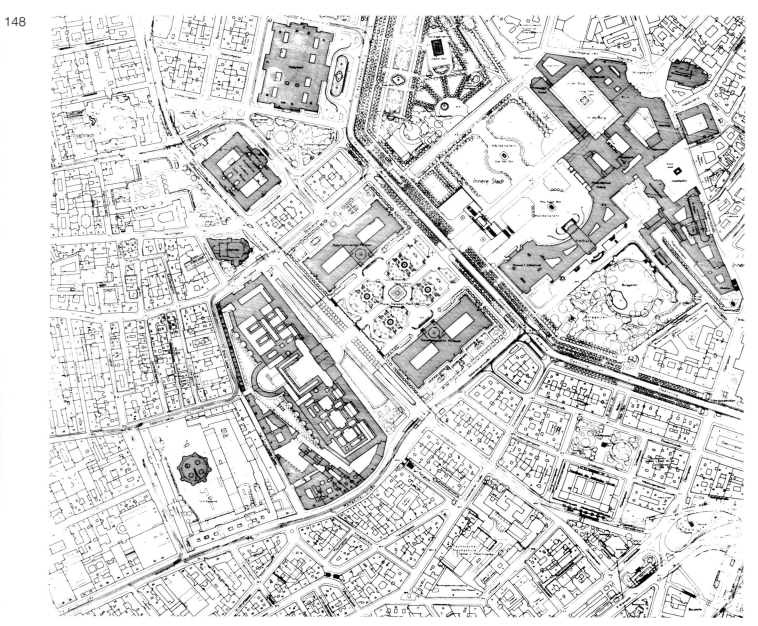

1

The competition site is contained by a long low range of buildings designed by Fischer Von Erlach that closes the northeast prospect from the Hofburg complex on the other side of the Ringstrasse. There are several existing pavilions of varying ages contained behind this range.
The range had to be retained but the existing buildings to it's rear could be removed.
The space to the front of the range is flanked by two buildings designed by Gottfried Semper—the Naturhistorisches and the Kunsthistorisches Museums.

The competition program required, as a first priority, the inclusion of a museum of modern art, an exhibition hall, and supporting facilities together with some public housing. The design also includes a museum for 19th-century art, a museum of photography, and the Leopold Gallery. The 19th-century galleries are placed at first floor level to the southeast side with large rooflit openings to the exhibition hall beneath. The Museum of Modern Art is placed to the northwest. The Leopold Gallery connects these and forms three sides of the entrance court. The disposition of the three main galleries allows exhibits to be

149

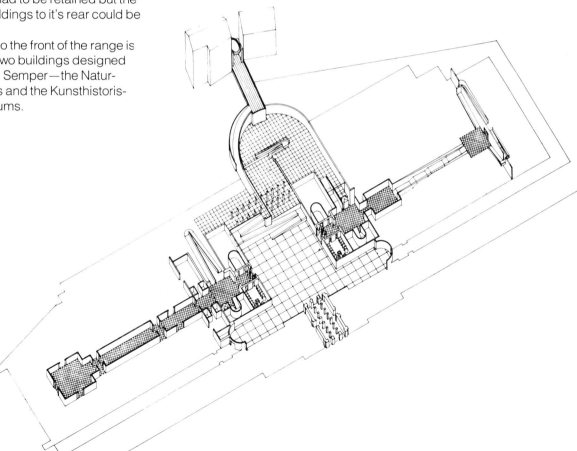

150 arranged chronologically. Service areas and plant are located at grade towards the rear of the site. The Fischer range contains general administration, The Vienna archive, the museum of photography, and the existing tobacco museum.

The rear of the galleries is lined with housing which screens the irregular backs of existing buildings lining Breite Gasse. Pedestrian access is provided from the entrance court to the housing district on the glacis to the rear of the site. This is achieved via a sequence of ramps below the Leopold Gallery. The final ramp follows part of the circumference of a semi-circular sculpture court and leads to a rear entrance on Breite Gasse.

The axis from the Hofburg terminates on a Second World War Flak tower situated on the glacis beyond the Messepalast site. This has suggested the displacement of the sculpture court to one side of this axis.

In order to integrate the Messepalast with the two Semper museums, Museumstrasse has been lowered beneath Maria Theresien Platz which has been extended up to the Fischer von Erlach building. This new underpass provides access to the car park.

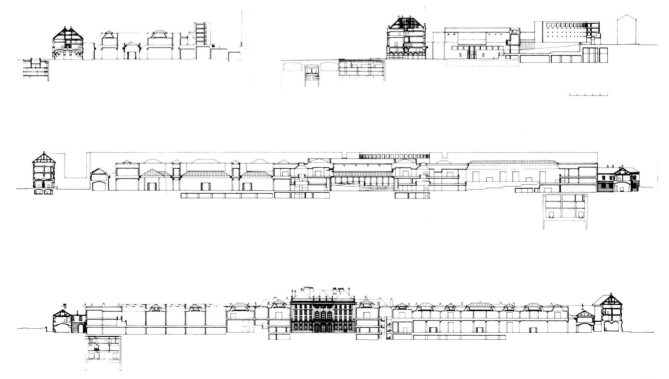

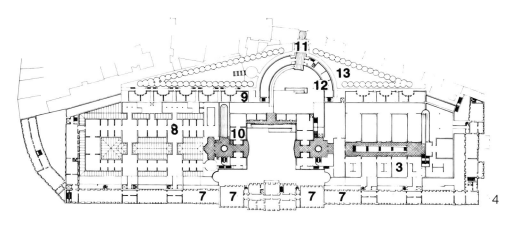

151

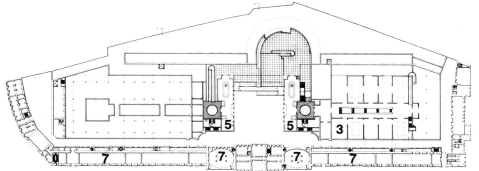

1 Entrance	6 Museums	11 Entrance
2 Exhibition	7 Administration	12 Ateliers
3 Museum of Modern Art	8 19th-Century Collection	13 Garden
4 Service	9 Residential	14 Underpass
5 Cafe/Restaurant	10 Leopold Collection	and Entry to Carpark

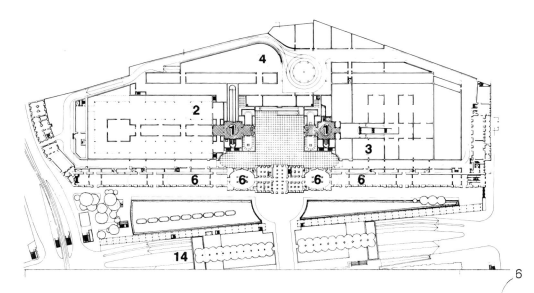